JEWISH THINKERS

General Editor: Arthur Hertzberg

Heine

Forthcoming titles in the series

BUBER
Pamela Vermes

RASHI
Chaim Pearl

BIALIK
David Aberbach

MENDELSSOHN
Arthur Hertzberg

ARLOSOROFF
Shlomo Avineri

BEN-GURION
Eli Shaltiel

WEIZMANN
Arthur Hertzberg

JUDAH HALEVI
David Goldstein

BA'AL SHEM TOV AND THE HASIDIC MOVEMENT
Ada Rapoport-Albert

IBN GABIROL
Raphael Loewe

AHAD HA'AM
Steven Zipperstein

MAIMONIDES
Amos Funkenstein

HERZL
David Vital

Heine

Ritchie Robertson

PETER HALBAN

WEIDENFELD & NICOLSON

LONDON

FIRST PUBLISHED IN GREAT BRITAIN BY
PETER HALBAN PUBLISHERS LTD
42 South Molton Street
London W1Y 1HB
1988

British Library Cataloguing in Publication Data

Robertson, Ritchie
Heine.——(Jewish thinkers series).
1. Heine, Heinrich——Biography 2. Authors,
German——19th century——Biography
I. Title II. Series
831'.7   PT2328

ISBN 1-870015-12-6

Typeset at Oxford University Computing Service
Printed in Great Britain by
Butler & Tanner Ltd, Frome, Somerset

CONTENTS

quoted from *Begegnungen mit Heine*, edited by Michael Werner (2 volumes, Hamburg, 1973), identified as W and volume and page number. Unless otherwise stated, all translations are my own, though I have profited from others' efforts and especially from the versions of Heine's prose in the various books by S. S. Prawer. In order to keep references to a minimum, the notes indicate the sources of quotations from writers other than Heine, and the sources of statistics cited, along with a few suggestions for relevant reading. Where possible, the reader is referred to accessible English translations of foreign works.

Heine has attracted a larger and finer body of English-language criticism and scholarship than any other German author, even Goethe. My immense debts to this corpus, especially to works by Robert C. Holub, S. S. Prawer, Nigel Reeves, and Jeffrey L. Sammons (listed under 'Further Reading'), will be patent to the informed reader; I have also profited particularly from the work of Albrecht Betz, Walter Kanowsky, Wolfgang Preisendanz, Dolf Sternberger, and Giorgio Tonelli. I am grateful to the editors of the *Cambridge Review* for permission to reprint some passages from my essay 'Heine, Hegel, and Shakespeare', and to Paul Connerton, Edward Timms, and Timothy Williamson for their painstaking and invaluable comments on drafts of this book. For all remaining defects I am alone responsible.

I

POETRY VERSUS POLITICS

Heine was a literary latecomer. When his first collection of poems was published, in 1821, the greatest period of German literature was approaching its end; its dominant figure, Goethe, was already in his seventies; and its established literary modes seemed almost worn out. The sense of the fragility of his literary materials is implicit, and sometimes explicit, in Heine's early poetry. A few years later he goes further and suggests that art itself is obsolete. 'The principle of the age of Goethe,' Heine writes in 1828, 'the idea of art, is in retreat; a new age, based on a new principle, is dawning' (1:455).

The age of Goethe annoys literary historians by refusing to fall into neat patterns. Its two main tendencies, Classicism and Romanticism, are sometimes opposed and sometimes interpenetrate. Heine's own writing is indebted in complex ways to both, though with Romanticism his love–hate relationship was particularly intense. By 1828, however, he felt that both belonged to the past, and for two reasons. Firstly, and more generally, they excluded modernity. Their underlying principles debarred them from dealing adequately with the complex and conflict-ridden modern world. Secondly, and more specifically, they excluded politics. They either ignored or obscured the political problems which had assumed a new urgency in the aftermath of the French Revolution and the Napoleonic wars. The main such problem, Heine came to feel, was the emancipation of mankind from political repression. By evading this problem, Classicism and Romanticism had become complicit in outworn and repressive political structures, and would perish with them. But if art could link itself to the new principle of emancipation, this new principle could ensure the survival of art, albeit in a new, rejuvenated form which by Goethean standards would not be recognizable as art at all.

Heine called the age of Goethe 'the period of art' (3:72) on the grounds that it was dominated by a conception of art as a separate and self-contained reality, without practical application and unsullied by politics. This separate aesthetic realm was mapped by Kant in his *Critique of Judgement* (1790). Kant argues that the beauty of a work of art, unlike that of a natural object, comes from its having been deliberately shaped; yet the work of art is not subordinate to any purpose, but is contemplated by the spectator with 'disinterested delight'.[1] Goethe uses the image of a balloonist to convey the serene, detached contemplation which art permits: 'True poetry is a secular gospel which announces its presence by freeing us, through inner serenity and outward pleasure, from the earthly burdens that oppress us. Like a balloon, it raises us and our ballast into higher regions, and affords a bird's-eye view of the intricate labyrinths of the earth below.'[2]

The aesthetic distance that permits serene contemplation is certainly one of the principles of the Classicism practised and promoted by Goethe and Schiller at the ducal court of Weimar. Heine acknowledges that Goethe's power of portraying objects solidly and vividly make his art truly classical. Hence he calls Goethe 'Wolfgang Apollo' and mocks the prudes who denounced 'the great pagan and his naked godlike figures' (2:219). But Heine also stresses that Goethe's works do not lead to action. Goethe's masterpieces, he writes, 'adorn our dear country as statues adorn a garden, but they are statues. One can fall in love with them, but they are sterile' (3:395).

Romanticism is conventionally opposed to Classicism. But while Heine often employs this antithesis, he also treats Romanticism as in some respects a continuation of Classicism. To see how this was possible, we must distinguish among three possible meanings of the word 'Romanticism'. Nowadays it refers to a Europe-wide movement of art and thought between roughly 1790 and 1830. For Heine, however, 'Romanticism' had the same meaning as for A. W. Schlegel, whose lectures on literary history he attended at Bonn University. It meant

Christian art of the Middle Ages and later, in contrast to the classical art of the Greeks and their imitators. When Heine calls himself the last Romantic poet, he means to invoke a thousand years of poetry, including Dante, Shakespeare and Cervantes, of which he is at the end. Thus he describes his mock-epic *Atta Troll* as 'the last free forest song of Romanticism' (4:570). And he writes (3.1.1846) to his friend Varnhagen von Ense: 'the thousand-year empire of Romanticism is at an end, and I myself was its last and fabulous king, who abdicated the throne.' The word is already used in this sense in one of Heine's first publications, the essay 'Romanticism' (1820), which paraphrases Schlegel: 'what is known as Romantic poetry, which flourished most radiantly in the Middle Ages, later withered away mournfully in the cold breath of religious conflicts, and recently has again sprouted from the soil of Germany and unfolded its most splendid flowers' (1:400). Here Heine is referring to the literary groups whom German literary scholarship, using the word in a third and much narrower sense, classifies as 'Romantic'. One group, centring on A. W. Schlegel, his brother Friedrich, Novalis and Tieck, came together in the university town of Jena in 1799–1801; another group, dominated by Achim von Arnim and Clemens Brentano, was based in Heidelberg between 1804 and 1809. Heine generally calls these groups 'the Romantic School'; this term becomes the title for the polemical study of German Romanticism which he published in 1836.

Even Heine's early writings show that he felt as ambivalent towards Romanticism as he did towards Classicism. If Classicism established a self-contained realm of art, Romanticism went further in the same direction by constructing a still more rarefied world. The formal garden of Classicism at least contained visible objects; Romantic art retreated into the inner world of the imagination. Although he praised Romanticism in 1820, Heine published in 1821 a verse dialogue, 'Conversation on the Paderborn Heath', in which a Romantic tries to defend his imaginative perceptions against the other person's prosaic common sense. When he claims to hear distant violins, bugles, shepherds' pipes, church bells, and other Romantic paraphernalia, the other explains them away as the grunting of pigs and

3

the tinkling of cow bells. Allowed the last word, the Romantic claims that at least the content of his heart cannot be dismissed as illusion. But this desperate move implies that Romanticism is an inward retreat from an unsatisfactory external world.

In thus criticizing the artistic possibilities of his day, Heine shows some points of contact with the aesthetic theories of Hegel. When Heine began studying at Berlin in 1821, Hegel was at the height of his fame as Germany's greatest philosopher, the living culmination of the revolution in thought initiated by Kant. Heine echoed the general opinion when in 1823 he called Hegel 'the profoundest of German philosophers' (2:87). He also claims to have known Hegel personally, though his anecdotes about him may be fiction. Despite Hegel's formidably difficult and abstract style, his lectures were thronged, and we know that Heine attended some. Although he complains of Hegel's style, his references to him are always admiring. In 1834 Hegel is emphatically described as the greatest philosopher Germany has produced since Leibniz in the seventeenth century (3:633). Even ironic references acknowledge his stature, as when he is called 'the Prophet of the West' (4:40) by analogy with Mahomet, the Prophet of the East. Since Heine's close friends included some of Hegel's most ardent disciples, it is safe to assume that from direct and indirect sources he had at least an outline knowledge of Hegel's philosophy, including the aesthetics.

In his monumental survey of art, Hegel argues that while for the ancient Greeks art could be the supreme expression of truth, in the modern world this task has passed to religion and philosophy. 'For us,' he writes, 'art counts no longer as the highest mode in which truth fashions an existence for itself.'[3] Tracing the history of art through Romanticism, he concludes by forecasting the dissolution of art in two ways. Art must surrender either to the objective world, by depicting everyday reality in faithful but unimaginative detail; or to the subjective world of the artist, by making the external world subordinate to his arbitrary fancy. The former possibility is represented, at its best, by seventeenth-century Dutch painting; the latter, by Sterne's *Tristram Shandy*.[4]

The danger of subjectivism, whereby art becomes confined to

4

the increasingly private imagination of the artist, was bound to concern a poet writing in the Romantic tradition, and it is explored several times by Heine. He examines it at most length in his fragmentary work of fiction *Florentine Nights* (1836), but touches on it more briefly, and for us more conveniently, in one of the reports on French cultural life which he wrote for German readers in the early 1840s. The mediocrity of the 1841 Salon, contrasted with the enthusiasm aroused by Liszt's concert tour, prompts Heine to a Hegelian excursus on the history of art. As Heine and Hegel tell it, art progressively detaches itself from material form and becomes more intangible, intellectual and abstract. Starting from the massive buildings, like the Pyramids, that survive from the ancient world, art passes through Greek sculpture and Renaissance painting to literature and music, which are almost entirely independent of their material medium. Heine declares that 'our present age will go down in the annals of art as the age of music' (5:356). For Heine, music is the most spiritual of the arts, in that it has no visual form and thus appeals to the mind rather than to the senses. As such, its utmost extreme is represented by the late Beethoven, who developed it 'to the musical death-agony of the phenomenal world, the annihilation of nature' (5:358). Heine thinks it significant that his deafness deprived Beethoven of the last thread of sensory contact with music, so that 'his notes were only memories of a note, the ghosts of departed sounds' (5:358). Such ghostly art might be a strange and sublime achievement, but one unthinkably remote from the turbulent realities of modernity.

In trying to confront the world around him, Heine ran the opposite risk: that of surrendering the imagination and capitulating before the sheer complexity of the modern world. Hegel describes how the modern world, unlike the simpler world of Homeric epic, resists the imagination. 'We must dismiss out of hand the idea that a truly epic action can take place on the ground of a political situation developed into an organized constitution with elaborate laws, effective courts of law, well-organized administration in the hands of ministers, civil servants, police, etc.'[5] Hegel therefore suggests that poetry is out of place in the prosaic modern world; epic poetry has given way to the novel, the epic of middle-class life. But if prose can describe the modern world, it does so at the cost of entanglement in mundane detail which debars it from any great artistic achievement.

At the outset of his career, therefore, Heine was faced with an obvious opposition between two genres of writing: poetry versus prose. Both literary modes presented dangers. Poetry had prestige as the accepted mode of literary expression; but it could imply retreating, as Heine thought Goethe had done, into a self-contained realm of art. Prose was frowned on as utilitarian; even the novel was not yet a fully respectable literary form. Most forms of prose writing—criticism, journalism, travel writing— were of still lower status. But they did provide ways of engaging with the modern world. And so we find the young Heine divided between prose and poetry. In his prose writings, above all in the *Letters from Berlin* (1822) and the *Pictures of Travel* (1826-31), he comments on the world around him with tireless interest and enthusiasm; while the poems of the *Book of Songs* (1827) convey nostalgia and regret for the past. But Heine was also working to reconcile this division, by bringing each side closer to the other. He introduced the everyday world of German society into his poems. And he made his prose much more than a workaday mode of communication, by giving it the imaginative richness and formal intricacy of poetry.

For Heine, the most genuine poetry was folk-poetry. Interest in folk-poetry had been aroused two generations earlier by Herder's essay *On Ossian and the Songs of Ancient Peoples.*[6] Herder maintained that the poetry produced in modern society was over-intellectual and artificial; vivid and vigorous poetry could be found only in the past, in Homer and Shakespeare, or among peasants and 'primitive' peoples as yet unaffected by the spread of civilization. By publishing a collection of folk-songs, Herder prepared the way for the famous collection of German songs, *The Boy's Magic Horn* (1806-8), made by Arnim and Brentano from oral sources and printed broadsheets. In *The Romantic School* Heine praised this collection extravagantly, though in fact Arnim and Brentano had never scrupled to adapt their originals to match their own notions of artless simplicity. They inspired a generation of German poets, including the young Heine, to refine the folk-song, keeping its spirit while removing 'the old awkward and clumsy expressions' (letter, 7.6.1826, to Wilhelm Müller, whose cycle of modern folk-poems, *Winter Journey*, was set to music by Schubert). Heine was not disturbed by the oddity of using artistic resources to achieve an effect of artlessness. But, despite some early successes in this line, he soon turned to a different kind of poetry. 'What matters,' he wrote in 1823, 'is to grasp the spirit of popular poetic forms, and with this knowledge to create new forms, adapted to our needs' (1:427). This meant using the language and imagery of folk-song but introducing scenes from modern society.

Heine's early poems were collected in the *Book of Songs*, which composers like Schubert, Schumann and Mendelssohn have made into Heine's most famous work. Throughout the collection, Heine presents what Hegel called 'the conflict between the poetry of the heart and the opposing prose of circumstances'.[7] But in case we expect Heine to retire from the unwelcoming outer world to the riches of his inner world, we have an early warning in the disillusioning poem 'Believe Me!', which catalogues Romantic clichés and concludes:

> But songs and stars and flowers by the ton,
> Or eyes and moons and springtime sun,
> No matter how much you like such stuff,
> To make a world they're just not enough. (D 45; 1:64)

Not only, therefore, is the real world at odds with Romantic visions; but the conventional material of poetry is too poor to create even a self-sufficient poetic world.

Many of the poems in the *Book of Songs* are love-poems, and most of these concern the misery of past or unrequited love. These have encouraged extravagant biographical conjectures. The scanty evidence suggests that in 1816 Heine was unhappily in love with his cousin Amalie and that this helped to inspire some of the love-poems, though admittedly most were written five years earlier. But two warnings must be given. Firstly: in the 1820s, unhappiness was a common literary attitude. *Weltschmerz* ('cosmic suffering') and *Zerrissenheit* ('inner discord') were clichés of the time. One can explain this by pointing to the fragmentation of modern society and the marginal role accorded to the poet; or one can note that problems about the purpose of life, and the justification of suffering, had lost none of their urgency, although the answers offered by religion were rapidly ceasing to convince. The resulting vacuum was described by Schopenhauer in the first volume of *The World as Will and Idea* (1819): all human striving results from a painful awareness of deficiency, but the satisfaction of one's needs produces satiety and tedium, so that all life oscillates between pain and ennui; hence man imagines hell as eternal pain, but heaven only as an eternity of boredom.[8] For Heine, the most influential exponent of world-weariness was Byron. He claimed a special affinity to 'my cousin Lord Byron' (letter to Rudolf Christiani, 24.5.1824), and translated passages from Byron's play *Manfred* and from *Childe Harold's Pilgrimage*, his poem of *Weltschmerz*. Byron's hero is already world-weary at the outset of the poem; his problem is that he has never had any illusions, but has always known that all happiness is deceptive and all human achievement transitory. His tour of the Mediterranean, taking in ruinous Rome and Turkish-occupied Greece, merely confirms his despair. Similarly, for Heine, disillusionment as a literary attitude is not the result of experience; it precedes experience. He knows in advance that reality will disappoint his expectations. The theme of unrequited love offers itself as a convenient vehicle for expressing such feelings.

Secondly, whatever impelled Heine to write it, the *Book of Songs* is structured as a work of fiction. This is clearest in the second section, *Lyrical Intermezzo*. Here we can discern a narrative in which the beloved proves to be deceitful, malicious, and coldly indifferent, marries someone else, and is miserable (or so the narrator hopefully surmises). Whether or not these events really happened, Heine needs this narrative to let him introduce more complex emotions and a recognizable social world. At their frosty final parting, the girl makes 'the politest of curtseys' (1:85); her marriage entitles her to be called 'Madame' (1:86); and the speaker's fantasies about his head serving as her footstool, his heart as her pincushion, and his poem as her curl-paper (1:88) serve, like the description of Belinda's dressing-table in Pope's *The Rape of the Lock*, to suggest someone chiefly concerned with primping and preening herself. The famous 'They sat and drank at the tea-table' presents ladies and gentlemen uttering sentimental or moralistic clichés about love; the poet reflects that if his beloved had been present, 'you would have talked so prettily, my darling, about your love' (1:96). Would she have shamed their triviality, or shared it? Heine leaves the conclusion ambiguous.

Much of the *Book of Songs* simultaneously exploits and questions the language of Romanticism. But the two cycles entitled *The North Sea* which round off the collection are Heine's response to Classicism. They attempt to incorporate into verse the intellectual content normally presented in prose, while avoiding the arid abstractness of much eighteenth-century philosophical poetry. They are in free verse, a form used in mythopoeic poetry by the young Goethe, and one of them, 'The Gods of Greece', is evidently a reply to Schiller's philosophical poem of the same title. Free verse creates more elbow-room than the neat quatrains or even the occasional iambic pentameters used earlier in the *Book of Songs*. It suggests the surging of the sea which is the setting for all these poems. Their title recalls Heine's visits in the summers of 1825–7 to Norderney, one of the East Frisian Islands. *The North Sea* appealed strongly to Heine, and on its shore he read Homer, whose verse provided another major literary inspiration for this cycle.

The North Sea deploys the Homeric gods in myth-making exercises in which we see Heine's imagination stretching itself, so to speak, and feeling its power. He imagines himself writing his beloved's name across the sky with a Norwegian pine-tree dipped in the fires of Etna, and communing with the gods to the extent of receiving a 'coarse sailor's jest' from Poseidon (1:186). But the dangers of the imagination are acknowledged too, in 'Sea Ghost': gazing at a drowned city beneath the waves, the poet recognizes his beloved and is about to plunge overboard when the captain pulls him back to safety and reality with a cry: 'Doctor, are you off your head?' (1:194).

In other ways, too, the imagination can mislead or betray one.

In 'The Gods of Greece' the clouds assume the shapes of the Greek gods who, banished by Christianity, now wander as ghosts through the night sky. The new gods, Heine reflects, are inferior, 'malicious in the sheep's clothing of humility' (1:207). As he meditates the gods fade away and 'in the sky the eternal stars emerge victorious'. This hints that Christianity too will have its day; all religions are transitory, and their myths and theologies merely try to conceal the unfeeling power underlying them. In 'Questions', a young man beseeches the sea and stars to 'answer the riddle of life' (1:208); but the sea continues to murmur unintelligibly, the stars are cold and indifferent, and 'a fool waits for an answer'. This anticipates the much more urgent and bitter questioning to be found in Heine's late poems. But for the time being Heine's imagination had reached a dead end. Mythopoeic poetry was futile in a demythologizing age, when authority had passed from myth and religion to science and philosophy and when, as Schiller wrote in 'The Gods of Greece', 'like the lifeless beat of the pendulum clock, nature, deprived of her divinity, slavishly obeys the law of gravity.'[9] Why beat one's forehead against the unanswerable cosmic problems when there were enough problems down on earth?

These problems, moreover, could be explored in prose without sacrificing the poetic imagination. We can see Heine trying out prose techniques in the *Letters from Berlin*. These light, chatty letters describe Berlin from the viewpoint of a *flâneur* pointing out the sights to a visitor. Heine asserts the supremacy of the imagination by stating the principle that 'association of ideas must always prevail' (2:10): thus his gaze moves rapidly from the musical academy to a tempting prostitute, thence to the bemedalled officers who throng the streets, to a café and a cake-shop. Though his interests are those of a leisured tourist, the *Letters from Berlin* point forward to Heine's mature prose. The technique of juxtaposition is already gently ironic, as when Prussian officers, placed between prostitutes and cafés, become just another tourist attraction; later, as in Heine's description of London, this technique will reveal what ordinary tourists overlook, by juxtaposing banks and crossing-sweepers. The

authority claimed by the narrative persona, here used capricious-
ly, will later enable Heine to practise a fast-moving political
criticism.

In *The Harz Journey* (1826), the first of his *Pictures of Travel*,
Heine brilliantly succeeds in linking the Romantic world of
legend with the preoccupations of a modern intellectual, and in
enlarging the scope of prose. Its model is Sterne's *Sentimental
Journey* (1768). Heine shares Sterne's wit and irony, and his
associative leaps (already tried out in the *Letters from Berlin*); but
he deepens Sterne's sentimental emotionalism into a heartfelt
response to nature, to legend, and to the qualities of German
working people. *The Harz Journey* is also an inquiry into the
German character, conducted by a German Jew; and, as we shall
see in Chapter 4, Heine in the early 1820s was feeling with
particular intensity the ambiguity arising from his dual allegiance
to a German and a Jewish identity.

The book recounts a walking tour Heine made in September
1824 through the Harz mountains, starting from Göttingen,
where he was completing his law degree. It contrasts two sides of
Germany. One side is the petty philistinism of the Göttingen
townspeople and the pedantry of Heine's professors, summed up
in the famous sentence (parodying the language of law
textbooks): 'For the most part the inhabitants of Göttingen are
divided into students, professors, Philistines and cattle, which
four classes are by no means sharply distinct' (2:104).[10] Heine
repeatedly mocks the unimaginative rationality of such people as
the 'well-fed citizen of Goslar' who asserts that everything in
nature is useful, e.g. trees are green because green soothes
people's eyes. Lacking true feeling, such people make do with
shallow sentimentality, like the young merchant who bursts out:
'How beautiful nature is, for the most part!' (2:145) The other
side of Germany is embodied in the narrator himself: he exhibits
his feeling for nature in descriptive passages interwoven with
poems and Romantic legends; and he encounters the real
German people when he visits a mining community and
descends a silver mine (described with a vivid realism new in
German prose). The steady, unchanging, contemplative life of
working people, he says, nourishes the imagination and has

produced the German folk-tale; Heine admired the tales which the brothers Grimm had published in 1812.

The high point of Heine's Harz journey, in both senses, is his ascent of the Brocken, the mountain famous in German legend and literature. Here witches were supposed to gather on St Walburga's Night (30 April), and their sabbat had been described in a scene of Goethe's *Faust*, which for Heine and many contemporaries was the outstanding work of German literature. This is one reason why Heine declares: 'The Brocken is a German' (2:142); another is that it lets one view the surrounding landscape with the pedantic thoroughness which is the other side of the German character. This side is represented by the crowd of students and other visitors whom the narrator finds in the inn on the summit of the Brocken. They spend an evening drinking and become increasingly fuddled; finally two students open a cupboard, mistaking it for the front door, and declaim highly literary rhapsodies to the starlit night, while the narrator retires to bed and dreams that he is watching an opera about Roman law. This rounds off the symmetry of Heine's narrative. At its lowest point, the descent into the mine, he escapes altogether from the pedantry and sentimentality of Göttingen and encounters the German people with their myth-making imagination. At its highest point, the Brocken, the mentality of Göttingen is turned upside down in a wild carnivalesque parody.

In *The Harz Journey* Heine takes a semi-literary genre, the travel report, and makes it into a superb work of art. Thus he has extended the scope of art, while steering clear both of the self-contained aesthetic realm and of Byronic world-weariness, and plunged himself into the everyday world. Heine mocks the cliché of world-weariness in *The Baths of Lucca* (1830). Here the narrator laughs at Gumpelino, a nouveau-riche businessman who prides himself on his cultivation, for declaiming sentimental verses about moonlight while gazing at a sunlit Italian landscape. Gumpelino responds crossly: 'You have no feeling for pure nature – you are a divided [*zerrissen*] man, a divided temperament, as it were, a Byron' (2:405). The narrator then comments on this, for the reader's benefit: such inner division is not just a psychological quirk, as Gumpelino suggests. In antiquity the world was whole; but now it is fractured, and since the poet is the centre of the world, the fault line runs through the poet's heart. It is pointless, therefore, for the poet to try to escape to a separate aesthetic realm. Placed by his vocation at the centre of the conflicts of his age, he is uniquely qualified to report on them. But he cannot remain a mere reporter. He also has to bear the responsibilities of his age by taking part in the political struggle.

Heine formulates the poet's responsibility in a passage from the *Pictures of Travel*. On his way from Munich to Genoa, at sunrise, his coach crosses the battlefield of Marengo, where Napoleon defeated the Austrians in 1800. Recalling how Napoleon vanquished the ancient regimes of Europe, Heine reflects on the new responsibility of the post-Napoleonic age. 'But what is the great task of our age?' he asks, and promptly answers:

> It is emancipation. Not only that of the Irish, the Greeks, the Frankfurt Jews, the blacks in the West Indies and such oppressed peoples; it is the emancipation of the whole world, especially of Europe, which has come of age and is now tearing itself free from the iron leading-strings of the privileged class, the aristocracy (2:376).

The writer, in Heine's view, had a special contribution to make to emancipation. Through the influence of their writings, the thinkers of the French Enlightenment had shaped the course of the French Revolution. Instead of being a mere sordid struggle for material benefits, the Revolution had pursued the ideal goals of liberty, fraternity and equality. 'Our age is warmed by the idea of human equality, and the poets, who as high priests do homage to this divine sun, can be certain that thousands kneel down beside them, and that thousands weep and rejoice with them' (1:432).

In Germany, however, liberty and equality had made little headway. While Heine was still a child, Napoleon's invasion had swept away the decaying Holy Roman Empire and most of the

hundreds of principalities it included. The region around
Düsseldorf, where Heine was brought up, was transformed by
Napoleon into the Grand Duchy of Berg, a French state
governed by the Napoleonic Code and with a written constitution. However, although he defeated the Austrians at Ulm and
Austerlitz in 1805, and the Prussians at Jena in 1806, Napoleon
failed to introduce liberal institutions into the rest of Germany.
In 1813, once Napoleon had been obliged to retreat from Russia,
Prussia proclaimed a war of independence. To gain popular
support, the war was presented as a national campaign waged by
the entire German people to free themselves from a tyrant.
Hence it was supported by liberals, who hoped that Germany
would become a national state with free institutions of its own.
But the war was also intended to restore the German monarchs
to the rights they had enjoyed before Napoleon's invasion, and
hence it appealed also to conservatives. The war was carried on a
wave of nationalist feeling, illustrated, for example, by Kleist's
German Catechism, in which a father instructs his son to regard
Napoleon as 'a parricidal spirit risen from hell' and any German
who fails to join in the national struggle against Napoleon as a
traitor.[11] The Prussian F. L. Jahn organized a gymnastic
movement to train young men in fighting and to inculcate
revolutionary nationalism. After Napoleon's defeat at the battle
of Leipzig in 1813, patriotic student societies (*Burschenschaften*)
were founded in the universities to preserve the spirit of the war
of liberation.

The aims of liberals and conservatives were incompatible, and
the latter triumphed. After the defeat of Napoleon, the chief
European powers gathered at the Congress of Vienna to restore
the status quo. Fearing that a united Germany might give scope
to revolutionaries, they set up a loose 'German Confederation',
consisting of 36 states and three free cities, which met in a Diet
(*Bundestag*) but retained their sovereignty. Its main architect was
Metternich, who was foreign minister of Austria from 1809 to
1848 and its chancellor from 1821 to 1848, and who was
determined to suppress revolutionary ideas. Most of the German
states were absolutist, without a constitution. Only the major
South German states were constitutional, with representative

government. The King of Prussia had promised his subjects a constitution in 1815, but in 1823, fearing that constitutional government might be the thin end of a wedge opening up the horrors of revolution and democracy, he withdrew his promise, and Prussia remained an absolute monarchy for another quarter-century.

German society was pre-industrial and politically backward. The political élite was formed by the aristocracy, who enjoyed preference in army and civil service. In the middle class, civil servants with academic training were sufficiently numerous and prominent to form a distinct group, with legal and fiscal privileges. Together with professional men and Protestant clerics, they formed the *Bildungsbürgertum* (educated middle class). Further down the social scale, the bulk of the German middle class consisted of artisans and merchants inhabiting small or medium-sized towns. In 1800 the three largest towns were Vienna, with 247,000 inhabitants; Berlin, with 172,000; and Hamburg, with 130,000. More typical were Aachen, with 27,000; Stuttgart, with 18,000; and Düsseldorf, Heine's birth-place, with 10,000.[12] Middle-class society was intensely conservative. Townsmen were organized in craft guilds which governed most aspects of economic and social life. They valued hard work, thrift and modest comfort; solidarity rather than competition; strict morality and an authoritarian family structure. Their political horizon did not extend beyond the town council: national politics were left to their betters.

In the universities, however, there were some liberals who demanded constitutional government, representation by popular assembly, freedom of the press and of association, and equality before the law. Liberalism was often associated with nationalism. Hence, after a political assassination by a student in 1819, a secret session of the Diet passed the Carlsbad Decrees to bring academic liberals and nationalists to heel. Lecturers were expected to submit the text of their lectures beforehand and not to deviate from the text. Academics suspected of revolutionary sympathies were dismissed. Newspapers and periodicals were brought under rigid censorship. The *Burschenschaften* were dissolved, though they survived illicitly. As soon as he arrived at Bonn University (the first of the three he was to attend) in 1819, Heine defied the decrees by taking part in a torchlight procession to commemorate the battle of Leipzig, and in 1820 he joined a *Burschenschaft*. The Carlsbad Decrees were effective in damping down political activity until 1830, when the July Revolution in France provoked some (mostly minor) upheavals in Germany.

Heine belonged on the radical wing of liberalism, though in the 1820s his ideas about politics were not fully formed and, as we shall see, his political stances were always individual and qualified. Besides joining a *Burschenschaft*, he deplored the fragmentation of Germany, and shared the nationalists' admiration for the ancient Germanic chieftain Arminius who defeated the Romans in AD 9 (W 1:66-7); nevertheless, Heine was not a German nationalist. Indeed he came to hate the nationalists bitterly because their construction of a 'Christian German' identity explicitly excluded Jews. He adhered to the ideals of the French Revolution, formulated in the Declaration of the Rights of Man and of the Citizen of 1789. He wanted the aristocracy swept aside, the power of the middle classes curbed, and political freedom extended to the people. But this does not mean that he wanted representative democracy. 'The people' (*das Volk*) was an emotional term, but also a vague and slippery one. The *Volk* suggested the hard-working backbone of the nation, unfairly denied political representation; but it could also suggest the impoverished masses who were not yet ready for full political rights. Hence few German liberals advocated even universal male suffrage; and Heine, as we shall see, thought autocracy acceptable if the autocrat genuinely represented the interests of the people.

Heine's political attitudes are implicit in *The Harz Journey*. The pettiness and affectation of the middle classes are contrasted with the generous spirit of the miners. While noting their loyalty to their king, Heine hints that it is naïvely misplaced, since Hanover, the state where the miners lived, was under British rule and its resident potentate was the Duke of Cambridge. Heine also works in an allusion to the ideals of the American and French Revolutions. When the narrator descends the mine, he does not penetrate as far as 'the lowest depth, where some say you can hear people in America shouting "Hurrah for Lafayette!" ' (2:116) The Marquis de Lafayette had earned the sobriquet 'the Hero of Two Worlds' by fighting against the British in America, and by supporting the French Revolution. In 1824, when Heine toured the Harz, Lafayette was on a visit to America where he was being enthusiastically welcomed. Heine seems to be suggesting that deep in the hearts of the German people, deeper even than their loyalty to their rulers, there is a devotion to freedom.

Such devotion to freedom was hard to find among German writers. Living at the end of the great age of German literature, Heine looked back at it through a political lens, to see what writers had done with their influence. His chief study of German literature is *The Romantic School*, which was written for the benefit of French readers. Heine finds that the political interests and the cosmopolitanism of the great eighteenth-century writers have been lost. The writer he particularly praises is the dramatist, critic and theological controversialist G. E. Lessing. Lessing, the first professional man of letters in Germany, an attractively forceful and witty writer and a champion of the Enlightenment, was evidently an important model for Heine. Indeed, Heine claims that Lessing is his favourite writer in the whole of world literature; and though this sounds extravagant, the records of his borrowings from the Düsseldorf library confirm that as a young man he read Lessing intensively.

Heine also praises Goethe for the political content of his early works, mentioning especially the incident in *The Sorrows of Young Werther* (1774) where Werther, as a commoner, is dismissed from a gathering of nobles. But although in the 1820s Goethe, despite his age, was as active as ever, he took no interest in the struggle for emancipation. Part II of *Faust*, which Heine found unintelligible, seemed to show that Goethe was devoting himself to a hopelessly esoteric form of art. Hence Goethe was attacked from both left and right for his political indifference, and for his supposed immorality and irreligion. The radical republican Ludwig Börne wrote: 'Goethe was mad on stability, and comfort was his religion'; while the Christian nationalist

Wolfgang Menzel called Goethe 'an aesthetic Heliogabalus' whose art, whatever its formal excellence, was frivolous, immoral, and apolitical.[13] Heine's own criticisms are much milder and more balanced than these, but they have a personal tinge. His Harz journey had ended with a visit to Goethe; we do not know what happened, but since Goethe was notoriously distant to callers, Heine probably found the visit a let-down or worse. There may be a covert allusion to this visit when Heine in 1828 compares Goethe to 'an old robber chief who has left his trade to lead a respectable middle-class life among the notables of a provincial town, tries scrupulously to practise all the philistine virtues, and becomes hideously embarrassed when he happens to meet some disreputable footpad from Calabria who wants to renew their old comradeship' (1:456).

If Goethe was indifferent to politics, Romanticism was worse: it was reactionary. The main targets of *The Romantic School* are the Schlegel brothers, for their reaction against the cosmopolitan and progressive ideals of the Enlightenment. Heine maintains that, despite their gifts as critics, they were unable to propose any new direction for literature; they looked back to the Middle Ages and advocated medieval poetry as a source of renewal for German literature. But this meant also praising the closed, hierarchical, religiously homogeneous society of the Middle Ages. They had little appreciation for more recent literature. They attacked Racine because, according to Heine, the sentiments of love and honour which animate Racinian tragedy too much resembled the feelings inspiring the followers of Napoleon. Even Shakespeare was too open-minded for them. Instead, they exalted the Spanish dramatist Calderón, whose plays are filled by an intense Counter-Reformation piety. A similar Catholicizing motive lay behind their Sanskrit studies. Friedrich Schlegel's epoch-making book *On the Wisdom and Language of the Indians* (1811) portrayed another closed society, to which modern notions of freedom were completely alien, and whose great epics depicted a conflict between kings and priests recalling that between Emperor and Pope in medieval Europe. And all this medievalism was intertwined with political reaction. Just as the Congress of Vienna tried to exclude liberal ideas from abroad by maintaining a closed, authoritarian society, so the Schlegels attacked Racine and elevated German folk-tales instead: 'Napoleon, the great classic, as classical as Alexander and Caesar, toppled to the ground, and the Schlegels, the little Romantics, every bit as Romantic as Tom Thumb and Puss in Boots, arose as victors' (3:380).

Heine continues his polemic by describing how the Schlegels' precepts brought forth a spate of Romantic dramas that tried to recreate the world of medieval Catholicism.[14] Indeed, Friedrich Schlegel himself became a Catholic, as did several other Romantic writers; while those who were already Catholics, like the philosopher Görres and the poet Brentano, adopted the most reactionary and uncompromising version of their religion. Meanwhile, in the hands of Görres and Schelling, German philosophy declined into obscurantism and irrationalism. And this deeply reactionary body of writing had been presented to French readers by Madame de Staël in *On Germany* (1813). Under the guidance of A. W. Schlegel, she depicted Germany as a land of profound and mystical poets and thinkers, and failed to mention its political backwardness and repressiveness. Elsewhere Heine portrays her, savagely but brilliantly, as an inquisitive interviewer, too self-obsessed to listen to answers, and so trivial that 'she regarded our philosophers as various flavours of ice-cream, and swallowed Kant as vanilla sorbet, Fichte as pistachio' (6:452).

The Romantic School was intended to counteract Madame de Staël's influence by explaining the political significance of German Romanticism. Heine's polemical intentions, however, do not prevent him from acknowledging the Schlegels' merits as critics and scholars. Nor do they lead to a wholesale demolition of Romanticism. *The Harz Journey* shows how deeply Heine sympathized with the Romantic tenet that a nation had its own spirit or soul (*Volksgeist, Volksseele*), and with the Romantic project of studying the expressions of a national spirit in history, folk-tales, myth and language. Jakob Grimm was not only a collector of folk-tales but a philologist inspired by Romanticism to compile the greatest German dictionary. Heine continues to affirm the value of popular poetry and folk-tales; and elsewhere he praises Grimm's dictionary as 'a colossal work, a Gothic cathedral, in which all the Germanic peoples raise their voices like vast choirs' (3:646).

But although Heine still enjoys folk-poetry and the Romantic lyrics of Eichendorff and Uhland, he tells us that he can no longer muster his former enthusiasm for such writing. He is now reading Uhland's poetry in Paris, at the centre of the modern world: 'The house where I am sitting and reading at this moment is on the Boulevard Montmartre, amid the roaring of the most furious waves of the present day, amid the screaming of the loudest voices of the modern age; there is laughter, rumbling, throbbing; the National Guard marches past at the double; and everyone speaks French. Is this the place to read Uhland's poems?' (3:486). Romantic poetry, Heine felt increasingly, was incompatible with modern life. 'The railway engine shakes and jolts our minds, so that we cannot produce a song; coal-smoke is driving away the songbirds; and the stench of gas-lamps spoils the fragrant moonlit night' (6:649).

To respond to modern realities, and promote emancipation, literature had to be politicized. In *The Romantic School* Heine holds up as models the Young Germans, a group of writers who 'wish to make no distinction between life and writing, who never separate politics from learning, art and religion, and who are at once artists, tribunes and apostles' (3:468). The Young Germans were not an organized movement but a set of writers who were radicalized by the tightening of censorship in the early 1830s. In trying to politicize art they were inspired by the prose works, like the *Pictures of Travel* and *Conditions in France*, in which Heine had confronted contemporary politics. Here, and to a lesser extent in the radical journalism of Börne, they recognized a new form of prose, enriched by imagery and irony. One of them wrote: 'It seems as though Germany's greatest poets are now to be found among the prose-writers.'[15] Heine returns the compliment by praising the Young Germans in terms which seem excessive, now that even the foremost among them, Heinrich Laube (who became a close friend of Heine) and Karl Gutzkow, are of interest mainly to literary historians.

Despite their liberal principles, the Young Germans took no

active part in politics. But in the Germany of the 1830s, any political comment was bound to get its author into trouble. The criticism of marriage and the (very tame) sexual explicitness in Gutzkow's novel *Wally the Sceptic* (*Wally die Zweiflerin*, 1835) provoked a decree from the Federal Diet forbidding the Young Germans, among whom Heine was included, to publish in Germany. This effectively silenced them as political writers. Heine, who had been living in Paris since 1831, was the least affected by the ban, partly because some of his writing was published in France and partly because his German publisher was adept at evading the censorship regulations. He found himself obliged to choose between expressing his opinions freely in some obscure magazine, or incompletely in a widely-read newspaper, and he chose the latter: hence his reports on French politics and culture in the 1840s were published with some mutilation in a leading German newspaper, the *Augsburg Gazette*.

Heine knew also that the need for security for oneself and one's dependants was a force urging caution. While still in Germany he wrote that, much as he would like to marry and set up a home, his lack of possessions ensured his independence. The ensuing flight of fancy is also a reflection on the subtle threats to a writer's freedom of expression:

I am quite annoyed with myself for having recently acquired a tea-set—the sugar-bowl was so alluringly gilded, and one of the cups had a picture of my favourite, the King of Bavaria, and another cup showed a sofa and marital bliss, beautifully painted... I already feel that the accursed china hampers my writing, I am becoming so tame and cautious, fear often drives me into flattery—in fact I shouldn't be surprised if the china salesman was an Austrian police agent and Metternich lumbered me with the china in order to tame me... But I am still strong enough to break my china fetters, and if my wrath is roused, then make no mistake, the whole tea-set, except for the cup with the King on it, will go out of the window, and anyone who happens to be passing had better look out for the splinters (2:627).[16]

This passage alludes to the attempt Heine made in 1828 to obtain a professorship at the University of Munich. And later in life the need for money did force him into compromises. Although, as we shall see in Chapter 3, he sharply criticized the French government, he received a pension from it; he tried to keep this secret, and was embarrassed when it became known after the 1848 Revolution.

In 1840 the accession of Friedrich Wilhelm IV to the Prussian throne, where his reactionary father had reigned for 43 years, aroused hopes of liberalization and unleashed a flood of political verse, much more radical than the writings of the Young Germans. One of these *Tendenzdichter* ('committed poets') was Ferdinand Freiligrath, who later went into political exile in London; another was the philologist Hoffmann von Fallersleben, who was dismissed from his academic post for political verse including the 'Song of the Germans' ('Deutschland, Deutschland über alles'), which is not always recognized as a liberal poem calling for a German national state with free institutions. Their poems were radical in content, but conservative and often pedestrian in form. Heine was annoyed by their flat-footed verse and banal sentiments. He later recalled:

> The Muses received strict instructions to stop their idle and thoughtless gadding about and to enter the service of their country, as camp-followers of freedom or washerwomen for Christian Germanic nationalism. In Germany's bardic grove there arose especially a vague, unfruitful ranting, a useless vapour of enthusiasm, that made a death-defying plunge into an ocean of generalities. It always reminded me of the American sailor who was so carried away by enthusiasm for General Jackson that one day he leapt from the mast-head into the sea, crying: 'I die for General Jackson!' (4:494)

What irritated Heine was the notion that political virtue could compensate for aesthetic slovenliness. And yet he too shared the tendency to radicalism and wrote a collection of pungent *Poems for the Times*. These include simple and vigorous calls for freedom (e.g. 'Adam the First', 4:412), but most are satirical, and Heine's satire faces in several directions. He denounces the German authorities, but also mocks the clichés of patriotism and the Germans' incapacity for revolution. The German princes, Heine suggests, have nothing to fear, because their subjects regard them with automatic and mindless loyalty:

> We always call them our Fathers, and
> We call their country our Fatherland,
> This ancestral estate where princes sprout.
> We also love sausage and sauerkraut. (D 405; 4:429)

The stridency of the political poets provoked Heine into asserting the claims of poetic genius over that of the party line. The genius belonged to an élite and was not to be constrained by the day-to-day demands of politics. 'Truly great poets have always responded to the great issues of their time in a quite different manner than in versified journalism; and they have been unconcerned when the servile crowd, whose vulgarity disgusts them, accuses them of adopting an aristocratic attitude' (5:438).

But Heine also suspected that the political poets were portents of the future. He foresaw a literature wholly subordinated to the demands of politics. In 1840 he published a harsh polemic against the recently dead Börne, charging that Börne had sacrificed his artistic conscience to his political loyalties, and had descended to a style which itself condemned his politics, full of 'metaphors whose mere shadow warranted twenty years' imprisonment in a fortress' (4:67). But in the egalitarian future proclaimed by Börne and his ilk, there would be no place for genius. Stylistic equality would be imposed on writers, compelling them all to write equally badly (6:662). He concluded his book on Börne on an elegiac note: 'The kings depart, and with them go the last poets' (4:141).

In his political satire Heine's model was Aristophanes, whose comedies had subjected well-known figures of ancient Athens to mockery which was sexual and scatological as well as openly political. At the end of his longest and most overt political satire,

Germany: A Winter's Tale (1844), he claims Aristophanes as his poetic father and warns the King of Prussia that maltreated poets can confer on their enemies an unwanted immortality. Heine was not alone in admiring Aristophanes. Many dramatists of the 1840s wrote Aristophanic comedies. But censorship made it impossible to stage these plays in their time, while their sedulous imitation of Aristophanes' elaborate metres blunted their satire and condemned them to oblivion. Heine, however, imitated not the metres but the spirit of Aristophanes by writing satire in verse.

Heine's fullest counterblast to the *Tendenzdichter* is the long satirical poem *Atta Troll: A Midsummer Night's Dream* (1841). Its eponymous hero is a dancing bear who breaks his chain and returns to his cave in the Pyrenees, where he is eventually hunted down. But this bald summary conveys nothing of the exuberance of Heine's writing. The poem exemplifies a mode of writing in which Heine excelled: the long poem in rhymeless trochaic quatrains, where the absence of rhyme permits an easy, conversational flow that can accommodate a leisurely narrative with frequent digressions and with unpredictable modulations of tone. The nearest equivalent in English (apart from rhymelessness) is Byron's *Don Juan*.

The satire of the poem is directed at a bewildering variety of targets. Most generally, the galumphing Atta Troll serves to satirize the Germans' roughness and stupidity. But he also embodies more specific kinds of folly. At times he represents the simple-minded political virtue which placed a sound character above literary talent, a criterion often used to depreciate Heine. Hence, after he has been hunted down and killed, his epitaph describes him as a *Tendenzbär* ('committed bear') who had 'no talent, but a character!' (4:563). Earlier, Atta Troll delivers a long speech expressing all the egalitarian doctrines that Heine found most worrying. Denying that any species is more gifted than another, Atta Troll proposes to found a state in which all animals shall be equal:

> Strict equality! Each ass will
> Have a right to highest office;
> On the other hand, the lion
> Will trot grain sacks to the mill wheel. (D 433; 4:511)

When Atta Troll is reunited with his cubs, Heine changes his target and makes them represent the loutishness of German nationalists. Later Atta Troll expresses the religious views of a German Philistine. Instead of the visionary religion that Heine sympathized with, as we shall see in the next chapter, Atta Troll conceives his God in his own image. He warns his cubs against atheism, and tells them never to doubt that the world is governed by a colossal polar bear, seated on a golden throne.

As a whole, however, *Atta Troll* is not just another and better political satire, but a more spacious work of the imagination than anything the *Tendenzdichter* were willing to tolerate. In his preface Heine claims that the rise of the committed radicals has made it imperative to 'defend the indefeasible rights of the spirit, especially in poetry' (4:495). Canto 3 of the poem begins with a ringing declaration of the autonomy of art:

> Summer night's dream! Full of fancy,
> Aimless is my song. Yes, aimless,
> As is love, as life is aimless,
> As Creator and creation.
>
> Heeding his own pleasure only,
> Whether galloping or flying,
> In the realms of fabled story
> Romps my dear-loved Pegasus.
>
> He's no serviceable cart horse
> From a virtuous burgher's stable,
> Nor a war horse neighing fiercely
> In the strife of party passions. (D 426; 4:501-2)

At the end of the poem Heine sums it up as the last Romantic poem, suggesting that the future lies with the *Tendenzdichter* and that future poetry will be dedicated single-mindedly to the political struggle. Atta Troll's lair is in Roncesvalles, where, according to the Old French epic poem *The Song of Roland*, the hero Roland made his last stand against the Saracens. This is where the 'thousand-year empire' of Romanticism began. The death of Atta Troll, which parodies this episode, is also the death of Romanticism.

But Heine is not setting up a melancholy, and potentially reactionary, antithesis between the freedom that the imagination enjoyed in the past and the political discipline to which it will be subjected in future. Nor, despite his protestations, is he really identifying the poetic imagination with arbitrary whimsy. *Atta Troll* differs from political poetry, not in giving free rein to fancy, but in an esoteric depth which, ironically, resembles the esotericism Heine complained of in the late Goethe. But he has not fallen into Goethe's indifference to politics, for this hidden layer of meaning is itself political. Through it, Heine hints that the true poet, unlike the *Tendenzdichter*, is in contact with powerful and permanent forces which will eventually sweep away the present-day radicals in their turn. This message is latent in the folk-tales and legends that Heine has incorporated into *Atta Troll*.

Heine was always fascinated by folk-tales and superstitions. In his *Memoirs* he tells a long and doubtless semi-fictional story about witchcraft he encountered as a boy in Düsseldorf. While on holiday on Norderney he collected local legends about witches who could control the wind and about the guardian spirit, the *Klabotermann*, who protected ships from the witches' malice. There too he heard the legend of the Flying Dutchman; he relates it in full in his unfinished novel *Memoirs of Herr von Schnabelewopski* (1834), where it was later found and adapted by Wagner. In Paris in 1833 Heine met the young Hans Christian Andersen, and heard his stories about Danish kobolds, the spirits (called brownies in Britain) who inhabited houses and would do housework if suitably propitiated. He read not only the Grimms' fairy-tales, but the collections of Germanic myths published by Jakob Grimm as *German Legends* (*Deutsche Sagen*, 1816-18) and *German Mythology* (*Deutsche Mythologie*, 1835). These and similar works provided material for his essay *Elemental Spirits* (1837), on the dwarfs, nixies, elves and salamanders which German folk-belief had assigned to the various natural elements.

But Heine's interest in folk-tales was not simply antiquarian. Like Jakob Grimm, he believed that they were remnants of the ancient Germanic religion. In being concerned with the natural world, this religion anticipated the pantheistic materialism which, as we shall see in the next chapter, Heine himself came to profess. The triumph of Christianity, however, had directed people's attention away from earthly realities towards a disembodied spiritual realm. Missionaries informed their converts that nature was evil and that the gods inhabiting it were really devils. Christianity also demonized the Greek gods, whose fates Heine recounts in *The Gods in Exile* (1853). It was particularly hostile to the goddess Venus, representing her as a she-devil who tempted men with her sensual charms, while Diana was said to have abandoned her chastity and to ride through the forests at night with the Wild Hunt.

In Heine's favourite works by Goethe and the Romantics, he found an alliance between great literature and the spirit of the German people. He admired *The Boy's Magic Horn* as a work in which 'one feels the heartbeat of the German people' (3:450). And he regarded Goethe's *Faust* less as a self-sufficient work than as a memorable version of 'the great, mystical German national tragedy of Dr Faust' (2:140). Unlike the German nationalists, who claimed that the Germans' deepest instincts were conservative, Heine, as we saw in *The Harz Journey*, preferred to think that the German people, deep down, were committed to freedom. His obvious course, therefore, was to adapt folk-poetry and folk-tales so as to bring out their latent revolutionary content, link it to the political programme of emancipation, and thus deprive the German nationalists of one of their most potent weapons.

Symbols of liberation, taken from Germanic legend, appear in *Atta Troll*. Three cantos describe the Wild Hunt, and Atta Troll is eventually shot by a mysterious character called Laskaro, the son of a witch. Laskaro, we are told, is really dead, but is given a semblance of life by his mother's magic. This enigmatic figure has perplexed commentators, but has recently been

27

plausibly interpreted by Nigel Reeves as representing the ancient Germanic folk-religion. Although believed dead, this religion is dormant in the depths of the German soul, and finds expression in folk-tales. Hence the link between Laskaro and the folk-tale figure of the witch; and this is also why the poet-narrator, with his imaginative insight into the German soul, accompanies Laskaro on the bear-hunt. Combined with the Germans' deep-seated desire for freedom, this folk-religion, if once restored to life, would be revolutionary, and we shall see in the next chapter what effects Heine ascribed to it.

However, Heine regarded revolution with mixed feelings, and his ambivalence is discernible in *Atta Troll*. The folk-religion, embodied by Laskaro, destroys the foolish revolutionaries, represented by Atta Troll, whose vision extends no further than the nineteenth century. But Laskaro is a sinister figure, haggard and silent. He resembles the muffled figure who appears in a dream-sequence of *Germany: A Winter's Tale* as the executioner whose deeds turn the poet's thought into action. By using such figures as symbols of political emancipation, Heine conveys a profound disquiet about revolution. The next chapter will show in more detail what Heine meant by the revival of the Germanic folk-religion, and how he incorporated this conception into an elaborate philosophy of history, in which the history of the world is interpreted as a conflict between the spirit and the senses.

2

THE SPIRIT VERSUS THE SENSES

Heine's conception of history has two main sources. One is Hegel, whose lectures on history Heine attended at the University of Berlin. The other is the French social thinker Henri Saint-Simon and his principal followers, whose writings Heine encountered later in the 1820s. Heine adopted Hegel's view of the structure of history, as gradual progress through conflict. But for his understanding of the content of history, of the issues at stake in history's many conflicts, he was more indebted to the Saint-Simonians. And while Hegel helped him to interpret the past, the Saint-Simonians also encouraged him to speculate about the future.

Heine attended Hegel's lecture series on the philosophy of world history in the winter term of 1822–3, as well as some of Hegel's lectures on the philosophy of religion. As we have seen, he probably also acquired an outline knowledge of the rest of the Hegelian system. This would be necessary, for Hegel's philosophy of history presupposes some knowledge of his main work, usually known in English as the *Phenomenology of Spirit* (1806). Its difficulties begin with its title. The second noun, *Geist* in German, can be translated as either 'spirit' or 'mind', and each version captures only half of Hegel's meaning. *Geist* is the larger force outside ourselves that may be sensed in moments of exalted feeling. Wordsworth's lines about 'a motion and a spirit, that impels / All thinking things, all objects of all thought, / And rolls through all things', convey something of its nature.[1] Hegel sympathized with the Romantics' view of the universe as a living spiritual organism, not a collection of dead atoms. But if we stress the Romantic side of Hegel's thought by choosing the translation 'spirit', we may invite misunderstanding. Unlike the

God of Christianity, this 'spirit' does not exist independently of mankind. To exist at all, it must realize itself, assume a form. And it realizes itself in a succession of different forms. First it is embodied in the physical world; then it finds an additional and more satisfying form in man, in the human mind. For this 'spirit' is also rational. Its nature is identical with the rational character of the mind, and it can best be understood through logic. Thus Hegel is only partially a sympathizer with Romanticism. He also follows the Enlightenment in asserting the supremacy of reason. But if we call *Geist* 'mind', we risk implying that it is only human consciousness writ large. In fact *Geist* is both 'spirit' and 'mind'. It is the force animating the world, and it is also the rationality which forms the structure of the human mind.

Since it realizes itself in stages, *Geist* has a history. Its two aspects, the human mind and the spirit animating the world, are separated, and *Geist* struggles to bring its two parts together. The *Phenomenology* is the story of this struggle. It is a narrative of the different forms of consciousness assumed by *Geist*. At its most rudimentary stage, that of 'sense-certainty', the mind dimly perceives the world but cannot yet form any ideas about it. Thenceforth the mind passes through various forms of alienation from the world until at long last the mind recognizes that the world and it are both aspects of the one *Geist*, and the two are reconciled. From this ultimate vantage-point, the reunified *Geist* can look back over the whole course of its previous development, and understand it fully. This vantage-point, Hegel believed, had been reached with the writing of the *Phenomenology*.

The history of *Geist* can be presented, as in the *Phenomenology*, as a spiral ascent through various forms of consciousness. But it can also be shown throughout the history of the world. 'The World-Spirit,' says Hegel, 'has had the patience to pass through these shapes over the long expanse of time, and to take upon itself the enormous labour of world history.'[2] In history, as in thought, the progress of *Geist* is not straight but dialectical. It takes the form of ideas which inspire people and nations. But, so long as *Geist* is divided, according to Hegel, people's ideas must always be incomplete. When an idea turns out to be incomplete and unsatisfactory, it must be combined with its opposite. The resulting synthesis preserves both poles of the opposition in a higher unity. But sooner or later this synthesis must in turn reveal its incompleteness and be combined with its opposite. How this works in history can be illustrated from the contrast Hegel draws between the religions of the ancient Greeks and the ancient Hebrews. The Greeks partially overcame the mind's alienation from spirit by imagining the gods in human form, as Zeus, Hera, Apollo, and so on. But in being humanized, the gods lost their universality and became only local deities whose writ did not run outside Greece. Meanwhile, the Hebrews imagined God as universal: Jehovah's laws were morally binding on all mankind. But the price of Jehovah's universality was that, unlike the Greek gods, he could not take on physical embodiment, but remained outside the world. These two opposites, each mirroring the other's incompleteness, were reconciled in Christianity. The Christian God is universal: his laws are valid for all mankind. But, unlike Jehovah, he has really entered the world, by assuming physical form as the individual person Jesus Christ. Thus Christianity is a dialectical synthesis of its Hebrew and Greek components.

Each nation—the Hebrews, the Greeks, the Romans, etc.—has its historical mission as the representative of an idea. Each plays its part on the stage of world history (which for Hegel is largely equivalent to European history): it develops one aspect of *Geist*, and is then replaced by its successor. The transitions in history are brought about by what Hegel calls 'world-historical individuals': those outstanding leaders, like Alexander the Great, Julius Caesar or Napoleon, who are driven on irresistibly to tear down an outdated historical structure and to begin building a new one in its place.

In recent history, the turning-points that Hegel picks out are the Reformation and the French Revolution. The decline of the Roman Empire allowed Christianity to conquer the world; but the price Christianity paid was that throughout the Middle Ages it became increasingly enslaved to the world. It paid more attention to material things, to church buildings and ceremonies, than to spiritual realities. Martin Luther's Reformation was needed to remind people of the spiritual basis of religion. But Luther did not turn away from material life. He insisted that the religious life should be led in the world, through marriage and work. However, his synthesis of spirit and matter was unstable. To establish it, he had to challenge the authority of the Church and maintain that every devout person was able to understand the teachings of Christianity. Thus, as well as exalting faith, he set up human reason as the arbiter of religious truth.

This synthesis held so long as reason was inspired by devotion. But in succeeding centuries reason became independent of faith. The philosophers of the Enlightenment cast a cool, scientific eye on the natural world, and tried to explain religion away as an intellectual error. In politics, Rousseau tried to construct a society based on absolute freedom. But when Rousseau's schemes were put into practice in the French Revolution, absolute freedom turned out to be empty. It could not be embodied in new political institutions; for any institution places some restraints on the freedom of the people who form it. Hence the ideal of absolute freedom could lead only to destruction: first to the destruction of the old order, then to the killing of human beings in the Reign of Terror. The section of the *Phenomenology* entitled 'Absolute Freedom and Terror' provides a philosophical underpinning for the modern truism that revolution, like Saturn, devours its own children.[3]

Like most thinkers of his generation, Hegel had greeted the French Revolution with high hopes. It seemed about to transform the world to match its ideals of liberty, fraternity and equality. Late in life he recalled:

All thinking beings shared in the jubilation of this epoch. Emotions of a lofty character stirred men's minds at that time; a spiritual enthusiasm thrilled through the world, as if the reconciliation between the Divine and the Secular was now first accomplished.[4]

The decline of the Revolution into a bloodbath disillusioned its supporters, much as in the twentieth century the hopes raised by the Russian Revolution were dashed by Stalinism. Instead of discarding the ideals of the Revolution, however, Hegel tried to work out a new political order which should satisfy man's desire for universal freedom and justice but realize these ideals in stable institutions and thus avoid the danger of revolution. Moreover, such a political order would embody the reconciliation of the divine and the secular, or rather of 'spirit' and 'mind', which Hegel saw as the goal of history. It would be the setting for a fully human life, in which man would at last be at home in the world.

Hegel describes this political order in the *Philosophy of Right*, and we must glance briefly at it, since it was Hegel's political thought that provoked many of his one-time admirers, including Heine, into creative disagreement. Once again, Hegel offers a dialectical synthesis. His conception of the state is intended to preserve the most valuable features of two incomplete social models: the family, and what he calls 'civil society'. With its warmth and intimacy, the family provides a setting in which people can perform their duties to one another out of affection, without any sense of compulsion. But the family is too simple to serve as a model for the complex relations within a large-scale community. A better model is civil society: that is, society as it was conceived by *laissez-faire* economists like Adam Smith. Civil society is an association of independent individuals, not linked by mutual affection, but only by common interests. Rather than duties, they have rights, which are enforceable by law. But civil society is too cold and impersonal to satisfy man's spiritual needs. Indeed, it does not even assure man's material well-being, for it tends to concentrate wealth in a few hands and reduce the masses to poverty. Hegel noted this happening in the industrially most advanced society of his day—Britain:

Despite an excess of wealth civil society is not rich enough, i.e. its own resources are insufficient to check excessive poverty and the creation of a penurious rabble ... In Britain, particularly in Scotland, the most direct measure against poverty and especially against the loss of shame and self-respect—the subjective bases of society—as well as against laziness and extravagance, &c., the begetters of the

rabble, has turned out to be to leave the poor to their fate
and instruct them to beg in the streets.[5]

The ideal political state retains the warmth of the family while
advancing beyond its simplicity, and retains the complex
organization of civil society without its uncaring egoism. This
state also overcomes the opposition between duties and rights.
The rights of the individual will be guaranteed by law. But
individuals will feel themselves to belong to a larger body, and
will gladly perform their duties towards it.

Hegel's reputation has always been haunted by the question
whether he believed that this state actually existed. Prussia was a
strong bureaucratic state which from 1807 onward had carried
out numerous liberalizing reforms. To some extent, therefore, it
conformed to Hegel's description of the rational state. But in
other respects it was far from Hegel's ideal. It was an absolute
monarchy, whereas Hegel envisaged a constitutional monarchy
in which the rights of the individual would be legally guaranteed. From 1819 onwards, moreover, Prussia slid into reaction.
As a professor at Berlin, Hegel was an official of the Prussian
state, and hence, by implication, an apologist even for its
repressive measures. To Heine and many others, Hegel seemed
to have sold out, becoming a 'state philosopher' who had donned
'the gleaming livery of power' (3:438). Both then and since, he
has been unjustly credited with the 'delusion that Prussia was the
embodiment of historical Reason'.[6]

Controversy focused on Hegel's famous sentence in the
preface to the *Philosophy of Right*, 'What is rational is actual and
what is actual is rational.'[7] Heine and many others interpreted it
as a complacent and self-serving defence of the existing political
order. Later, however, Heine revised this opinion, and concluded that Hegel's verbal obscurity and political caution had
been part of a far-sighted policy, designed to prevent the liberal,
indeed revolutionary, nature of Hegelian doctrines from becoming apparent too soon. Thus, in 1843, Heine deplores the
youthful folly with which he once attacked Hegel's conservatism
(5:498–9). And in one of his anecdotes about his acquaintance
with Hegel, he relates how Hegel told him, with a strange smile,

that the famous statement 'Whatever exists is rational' could also run: 'Whatever is rational, must exist.' The revolutionary implication of this version—that the world must and will be changed in accordance with the demands of reason—did not dawn on Heine until much later (5:197).

In this reinterpretation of Hegel, Heine was in agreement with the Young Hegelian movement which crystallized about 1840. These radicals condemned Hegel for defending as rational an existing order which was in fact unjust and therefore irrational. But they thought that the corrective to Hegel's conservatism could be found within his system. Hegel was right in saying that man must change the world to bring it into line with the demands of reason. He was only wrong in implying that this process was now complete. Properly understood, his philosophy yielded a programme for political action. Philosophy should criticize existing reality and guide people in the practical task of removing aristocracy, censorship and other irrational remnants of the past.

Moreover, the Young Hegelians blamed Hegel for getting lost amid philosophical abstractions. Instead of describing the self-alienation of *Geist*, he should have drawn attention to the self-alienation of man. Man was innately capable of happiness, strength and wisdom. But political injustice kept most people miserable, weak and ignorant. Unable to develop his innate powers, man projected them on to an imaginary being who was said to be omnipotent and omniscient. It was now time for man, through political action, to reclaim the qualities which he had projected on to God, and to enjoy the happiness which was his due.

In the 1840s these arguments were taken further and memorably formulated by the young Marx. The values projected on to God must be reclaimed and realized in human life: 'Man has found in the imaginary reality of heaven where he looked for a superman only the reflection of his own self.'[8] Philosophy must therefore issue in action. 'The philosophers have only interpreted the world, in various ways; the point is to change it.'[9] And German philosophy contains a programme for the future German revolution: 'We Germans have experienced our future history in thought, in philosophy.'[10]

All these claims, however, had already been made by Heine as early as 1834, in his longest essay in historical interpretation, *On the History of Religion and Philosophy in Germany* (henceforth referred to as *History*). This work complements *The Romantic School*, in which Heine had sought to explain to French readers the political significance of German Romanticism. Earlier still, in a polemic against the German aristocracy written in 1831, he had suggested that 'our German philosophy is the dream of the French revolution' (2:655). In *History* he now explains in detail the political significance of the German revolution in philosophy, from Kant to the present; and he traces the antecedents of this revolution back to the rise of Christianity. German philosophy, he asserts, is the prelude to revolutionary action: 'Thought seeks to become action, the word to become flesh' (3:593). And the goal of both thought and action is to rescue mankind from its present impoverished and self-divided state and restore it to wholeness. He followed Hegel in seeing history as a story of conflicts. But in identifying the antagonists in these conflicts, and the way in which they might be reconciled, he was indebted to one of the visionary socialist doctrines that were being developed in France.

While still in Germany, Heine seems to have learnt of the doctrines put forward by Henri Saint-Simon and expanded by his followers. Saint-Simon proposes a new social order appropriate for an industrial and scientific age. At present, he warns, the exploitation of man by man keeps the proletariat in virtual slavery, while the inheritance of property maintains a privileged class of idlers. Such injustice renders a revolution inevitable. It is therefore necessary to plan for a new social order appropriate to an industrial and scientific age, with no hereditary distinctions of wealth or status. People should be assigned places in society according to their innate abilities, and rewarded according to their merit. Society will be divided into three classes: industrial workers (including administrators), scientists and artists. The latter two complement each other, for Saint-Simon thinks it would be disastrous for man's intellectual capacity to outstrip his capacity for emotion and sympathy. The latter will be sustained by the future religion, based on the brotherly love which Saint-Simon considers the essence of Christianity, and nourished and directed by artists, who therefore have an honoured place in Saint-Simon's utopia. 'In the great enterprise of working directly for the establishment of the system of public good, the artists, the men of imagination, will lead the way. They will proclaim the future of the human race. They will take the Golden Age out of the past and offer it as enrichment to future generations.'[11]

Heine first learnt about Saint-Simonism from expositions of the doctrine published in 1829 and 1830. These present Saint-Simon in awe-struck terms as the bearer of a third religious revelation, completing those of Moses and Jesus. Matter and sexuality are to be rehabilitated from the contempt they have suffered under Christianity. Women are to be emancipated. Casual and long-term sexual relationships are to enjoy equal respect. Artists are assigned a role similar to that of priests: by proclaiming their visions of the future, they lead mankind to new heights of civilization. Heine's response is in a letter to his friend Varnhagen von Ense (1.4.1831): 'I dream every night that I am packing my suitcase and travelling to Paris, to breathe fresh air, devote myself entirely to the sacred feelings of my new religion, and perhaps to be ordained one of its priests.'

It may be revealing that Heine qualifies his enthusiasm by attributing it to his dreams, for in reality the Saint-Simonians were decidedly eccentric. After Saint-Simon's death in 1825 they were led by an engineer, Prosper Enfantin, who had formally set up a new church with himself as the Supreme Father heading an elaborate hierarchy. Enfantin required his followers to believe that God had placed the destiny of the world in his hands, and they readily declared that God was incarnate in him. However, in 1832 Enfantin and his closest associates were prosecuted and briefly imprisoned for offending public morality, and thereafter the movement faded away. While it lasted, it disturbingly resembled such present-day phenomena as the Church of Scientology. What can Heine have made of it?

Heine arrived in Paris, where he was to spend the rest of his life, in 1831. We know that soon after his arrival he attended some Saint-Simonian meetings, and that he was friendly with several leading Saint-Simonians, including Enfantin, to whom Heine dedicated the French edition of his writings on Germany in 1835. He praises the Saint-Simonians in his preface to the French edition of the *Pictures of Travel* (May 1834). They are right, he says, in claiming that since the beginning of industrialization social relations have been based, even more than in the past, on the exploitation of man by man. And Heine shares their aim of erecting a new church in which all men shall be priests (2:677). Subsequent references to the Saint-Simonians, however, are few and unflattering. An undated entry in Heine's private notebook runs: 'How much God has done in order to cure the world's ills! In Moses' time he performed miracle after miracle, later in the form of Christ he was scourged and crucified, finally in the form of Enfantin he made the ultimate sacrifice on the world's behalf: he made himself ridiculous' (6:625).

It is probably safe to assume that Heine took the doctrine more seriously than he did its doctrinaires. Saint-Simonism proposed to help the poor, to make social distinctions depend entirely on merit, and to give the artist an honoured place in society. All this, not least the third item, would appeal to Heine. In May 1832 he wrote to Varnhagen expressing the hope that the Saint-Simonians' doctrine might pass into wiser hands than theirs. 'As far as I am concerned,' he continues, 'I am interested only in the religious ideas, which needed only to be uttered in order to be realized sooner or later.'

Saint-Simonism could fuse with Heine's Hegelian teachings the more easily, because it had its own theory of history. It saw an alternation between organic ages, in which all human activities are based on a generally accepted theory and have a common purpose, and critical ages, in which society disinte- ates into a mass of isolated and quarrelling individuals. The Christian Middle Ages had been an organic period; the Saint- Simonians hoped to make their doctrine the basis for another. But Saint-Simonism differed from Hegelianism in having a utopian perspective on the future. Hegel asserts that philosophy cannot go beyond the possibilities presented by its own age; we can know nothing about the far future, and so it is folly to construct utopias. In a short essay dating from the early 1830s, Heine contrasts two theories of history. The view he prefers, in which history is seen as progress towards a future paradise, is recognizably Saint-Simonian. Heine contrasts this with the more pessimistic view of history as cyclical recurrence in which, as Ecclesiastes has it, there is no new thing under the sun, and observes that the latter view, in which progress is illusory, serves the purposes of conservative governments. But he also has a reservation about the utopian interpretation of history. Its adherents may be tempted to sacrifice the present for the sake of the future. But it is the present that offers each of us our only chance of happiness. One might say that the utopians' 'jam tomorrow' is no more filling than the conservatives' 'pie in the sky'. 'The starry-eyed prophets of a radiant future must not seduce us into jeopardizing the interests of the present and the human right that most needs upholding—the right to live' (3:23).

For Heine, as for Hegel, the chief actors in history are ideas. He justifies his own way of writing intellectual history by saying that 'facts are only the products of ideas' (3:466). And he describes Napoleon, in a letter to Varnhagen, as 'the man of the idea, the idea become man' (1.5.1827). In *History* he recounts a dialectical conflict between two ideas, for which he has various names. As they are associated respectively with the mind and the body, he calls them Spiritualism and Sensualism; and as one was most fully realized among the Jews of the Old Testament, the other in classical Athens, he calls them Hebraism and Hellenism. Each produces a different character-type. The Hebraic temperament is ascetic and fond of abstractions; though capable of brilliant sarcastic wit, it lacks good humour, and is inclined to gloom and severity. Hellenes, on the other hand, enjoy life, especially the pleasures of the senses; they do not theorize much, but are keenly interested in the world around them. History is the dialectical interplay between these two principles. 'For eighteen centuries now,' Heine writes, 'there has been a quarrel between Jerusalem and Athens, between the Holy Sepulchre and the cradle of art, between the spiritual life and the living spirit' (4:175).

Accordingly, the narrative of *History* and related works begins with the triumph of Christianity, the victory of Hebraism over Hellenism, of the spirit over the body. Heine then recounts the resistance by Sensualism, in a campaign whose battles include the Renaissance, the Reformation and the Enlightenment. These, as we have seen, are also the main landmarks in the somewhat different story told by Hegel. The philosophical revolution initiated by Kant is, Heine explains, the most recent of these battles; and its political consequences, he seems to suggest, will lead to the triumph of Sensualism in a decisive victory of the body over the spirit.

It must be stressed that although Heine favours Sensualism, the conflict between it and Spiritualism is not a conflict between good and evil. As in Hegel's dialectic, it is a conflict of two good but incomplete principles, each of which needs to enter into a synthesis with the other. Heine concedes, for example, that the rigorous spirituality of the Old Testament Jews was a necessary corrective to the gross sensuality of the ancient Orient; and the asceticism of early Christianity was likewise necessary to counter the brutish materialism of the Roman Empire. A perfect synthesis of the two principles is found in Shakespeare, whom Heine describes as 'at once Jew and Greek' (4:47). However, in his underrated essay *Shakespeare's Girls and Women*, Heine places more emphasis on the Hellenic, life-affirming, creative side of Shakespeare, for the sake of contrast with the dismal piety of the Puritans who closed down the theatres. Hence in *Atta Troll* both Goethe and Shakespeare take part in the Wild Hunt, the symbol of Sensualism; and both are found in the pagan paradise of Venus' cave in *The Goddess Diana*.

Heine's advocacy of Sensualism needs to be seen in a wider context. It is part of the tendency, dating from the eighteenth century, to locate man within the natural world, as a particularly complex animal. Christianity saw man as an immortal soul lodged in a perishable body. Kant saw man as simultaneously a rational being, with freedom of will, and a natural being, subject to the laws of the physical world. But increasingly it seemed possible to remove the painful conflict between the spiritual and physical sides of man by using the laws of nature to explain both.

Darwin's theory of evolution was to deprive man of his special status and return him to the animal kingdom; while Nietzsche and Freud were to describe man's mental life in the biological language of instincts and drives. Heine's Sensualism is another way of accommodating man within the natural world. But he presents it in two different versions. Sometimes he suggests that by discarding all pretensions to a spiritual nature, man will slip easily into harmony with the material world. At other times he proposes a dialectical reconciliation of the spirit and the senses, so that what is valuable in Spiritualism can be preserved within an earthly paradise. And his hesitation between these two solutions results, as we shall see presently, in a major contradiction in his view of history.

This hesitation is apparent in Heine's remarks on Christianity. Though Christianity may have saved our souls, it has enfeebled our bodies. 'Our age—and it begins at the cross of Christ—will be regarded as a great period of human illness' (1:545). In this passage—not from *History* but from *Memoirs of Herr von Schnabelewopski* (1834), which explores some associated ideas— Heine anticipates Nietzsche's view of spirituality in general, and Christianity in particular, as an illness which has deprived man of his former bodily health and made him into 'the sick animal'.[12] But, for a dialectical thinker like Heine, such illness brings benefits. Indeed Heine already formulates the idea that Thomas Mann was to explore in *The Magic Mountain* when, after contrasting the rude health of English tourists with the dignified pallor of Italians, he writes: 'Sick people are always more truly noble than healthy ones; only the sick person is human' (2:371).

Generally, however, Heine takes the side of health against illness. *Schnabelewopski* also contains a story about an Anabaptist truss-maker (an ironic symbol of the debility of the body under Spiritualism) who dreams nightly of encounters with Old Testament women like Esther, Judith and the Queen of Sheba, and eventually with the thousand women in King Solomon's harem. This story prompts Heine to reflect on dreams. Even if our dreams are less extravagant than the truss-maker's, their vividness shows how rigidly we have separated body from spirit. The ancient Greeks, Heine implausibly asserts, dreamt so little that any vivid dream was recorded. Real dreaming began among the spiritually inclined Jews and has reached its high point under Christianity. Heine is writing after a generation of Romantics had delved into the inner life revealed in dreams, visions and occult phenomena. Placing Romanticism in its social context, Heine has realized that the richness of the inner life is a compensation for the restrictions imposed by Spiritualism on the outer life. He thus anticipates Freud's concept of repression. And his programme for the restoration of Sensualism anticipates those neo-Freudians who have argued that by freeing erotic pleasure from the enclaves to which an exploitative civilization confines it, we may begin freeing ourselves from political as well as sexual repression.[13]

According to Heine's narrative, repression began when Christian missionaries confronted paganism. As we saw in the last chapter, the religion of the ancient Germans ascribed divinity to nature, which they imagined to be populated by elemental spirits. Heine now defines this belief as a form of pantheism: the belief that God is identical with the world, and hence that the world is itself divine. Hence he declares: 'Pantheism is Germany's hidden religion' ($3:571$), and finds versions of pantheism in the various Sensualist philosophers discussed in *History*.

The first of these philosophers is the Devil, for in the Middle Ages, the worship of nature and the other aspects of Sensualism condemned by Christianity became the Devil's province. Worldly pleasures were attributed to him, and legends show him feasting boisterously and presiding over sexual orgies at witches' sabbats. But Heine quotes Dante to the effect that the Devil is also a logician.[14] The Church, by insisting on blind faith, abandoned reason to the Devil. The Devil thinks for himself instead of trusting authority: hence he is condemned by the Church as the father of lies, but he also anticipates the Enlightenment. In the Spiritualist theocracy of the Middle Ages, the Devil was, so to speak, the perpetual dissident, helping reason and the senses to survive as an underground movement.

In particular, the Devil patronized dancing. Christianity tried hard to suppress dancing, recognizing in it a sensual revolt against ascetic discipline. More recently, civilization has tried to regulate dancing, especially in the form of ballet, but folk-dances continue to be sensual, even lascivious. In his reports on Parisian life in the 1840s Heine notes the return of open sensuality in the can-can, which, he claims, is thought so politically suspicious that dance-halls are watched by police agents. To Heine the can-can seems a cynical mockery of ideals; but it shows also that these ideals have become so degraded that cynical mockery is all they deserve (5:394). Heine illustrates this by contrasting the wild physicality of the can-can with the tedium of a respectable Paris ball. His account of the Middle Ages reveals a similar polarity. On the one hand, Spiritualism had almost lost contact with the world, as Heine illustrates by describing the vertical thrust of Gothic architecture in which 'everything strives upwards, everything is transubstantiated' (3:520). On the other hand, Sensualism could survive only in gross and brutish forms. In Heine's *Faust* ballet, the witches' festival is a crude parody of ecclesiastical ceremonies, and Faust finds both equally unpleasing. Thus each principle, unmixed with its opposite, sank into something poor and unsatisfying. A new synthesis was needed.

It was Luther who reunited the senses with the spirit. Heine depicts him as a complete human being, both mystical and practical, devout and pleasure-loving. His Reformation legitimized the senses by allowing priests to marry. Heine even tries to link him with pantheism by saying that as Luther's father was a miner, the boy might have felt the influence of the forces of nature in the depths of the mine. This relapse into the Romanticism of Novalis is untypical of Heine's good sense. One could also object that since Luther described the Mass as merely a commemoration, not a real manifestation, of Christ's presence, he might equally well be seen as separating sensory from spiritual realities. These oddities, combined with Heine's rhapsodic tone, suggest that Luther is being made to serve symbolic rather than historical purposes. He symbolizes the balance between matter and spirit allegedly attained by Protestantism.

After Luther, Heine's narrative bifurcates. Reason and the senses, reclaimed by Luther, now move apart and run along different though parallel lines. Along one line we have the rationalists who used reason to attack the intellectual defences of

Spiritualism. Along the other we find the pantheists who tried to construct a Sensualist philosophy for man to live by.

Let us follow the rationalist line first. After Luther had divided the Church, many theologians tried to enlist reason on the side of religion. They hoped that if the existence of God could be demonstrated logically, religion would be proof against any future attack. But, as Heine says, 'the moment a religion has to seek support from philosophy, its doom is sealed' (3:578). Religion needs unquestioning assent, not the flimsy support of rational conviction. The eighteenth century professed a bloodless Christianity which had been stripped of supernaturalism and reduced to a set of moral precepts attributed to a good man called Jesus. The supposed rational basis of this Christianity was sliced away by Kant. In his *Critique of Pure Reason* (1781) he argued that it was impossible to prove the existence of God, although Christian theologians had been trying to do so for centuries. Thanks to Kant, 'the last citadel of Christianity has been stormed, the garrison has surrendered, the Lord of the universe, unproved, is floating in his own blood' (3:604). Unfortunately Kant did not follow through his victory. In a later work, the *Critique of Practical Reason* (1788), he maintained that although God's existence could not be demonstrated, it had to be postulated as the foundation for moral conduct. Heine mocks this lamentable retreat by alleging that Kant made this concession out of pity for his old servant, who was distressed at no longer having a God to worship.

None the less, his demolition work made Kant into 'the great terrorist in the realm of thought' (3:595), the Robespierre of philosophy. Robespierre executed the King of France; Kant killed God, and in a mock-elegiac passage Heine looks back on God's progress, from its lowly start in Egypt via Palestine to the peak of his career in Rome, and its subsequent decline:

> We saw how he became yet more spiritual, how he whimpered mildly, how he became a loving father, a friend of mankind, a universal benefactor, a philanthropist —none of it helped him—

Do you hear the bell ringing? Kneel down—They are bringing the sacraments to a dying God (3 : 591).

In Nietzsche's better-known version of this theme, the death of God sends the earth careering out of its orbit and away from the sun into the freezing darkness of unknown space.[15] Heine takes no such nihilistic view of the consequences of God's demise. But he does see that reason is an instrument of destruction which, having battered down the world of Spiritualism, cannot itself construct a new world for humanity to inhabit. The materialism which dominated eighteenth-century thought in France and Britain cannot be used for reconstruction. It sees the world scientifically as a well-functioning mechanism, and its view of man, Heine says, is summed up in the title of the book by the philosopher La Mettrie, *L'Homme machine* (*Man the Machine* [1747], 3:557). Even the Saint-Simonians are too much influenced by this materialism. But their essential doctrines, which acknowledge mankind's spiritual needs, can flourish better in Germany, the homeland of pantheism.

The second intellectual track followed in *History* is the line of pantheist thinkers. The genealogy Heine constructs begins with the seventeenth-century Dutch-Jewish philosopher Spinoza. In Spinoza's thought, God and nature (i.e. the world) are the same thing. For the young Goethe, Spinoza's pantheism seemed to confirm his intuitive sense of the unity of humanity and nature and the presence of God within, not outside, the world. Hence Heine is justified in calling Goethe 'the Spinoza of poetry' (3:618). Pantheism is unaffected by Kant's victory over God, for Kant was concerned with the conception of God as existing outside the world; but if God is the world, then his existence is as tangibly certain as that of the world. Among the post-Kantian philosophers, pantheism had resurfaced in the philosophy of nature put forward by Schelling, whose lectures Heine had heard and enjoyed in 1828 in Munich. Schelling appealed to Goethe and the Romantics by articulating their intuitive sense of nature as vital, divine and animate. Rejecting the materialist view of an inanimate nature set over against an isolated, self-sufficient human mind, he insists that nature and the human mind spring from the same source. Far from being an object, nature is, potentially, a subject, a bearer of consciousness. Although its consciousness is still dormant, it is like a restless sleeper, struggling towards the waking state; while the consciousness borne by human beings longs to be reunited with nature. 'Nature must become visible spirit, spirit must become invisible nature.'[16]

An important passage from *History* paraphrases this view of nature as striving to become conscious and fuses it with Spinoza's equation of nature and God:

> God is identical with the world. He manifests himself in plants, which lead an unconscious life, in tune with the magnetic forces of the cosmos. He manifests himself in animals, which are more or less dimly conscious of their own existence. But he manifests himself most gloriously in man, who can at once feel and think, who can distinguish himself as an individual from objective nature, and already has in his rational mind the ideas which are revealed to him in the phenomenal world (3:569).

This may sound remote from the political interpretation of German philosophy which Heine promised his readers at the beginning of *History*. But in the same paragraph he draws on Hegel to show that pantheism is a dynamic historical force. God manifests himself not only in nature and man, but also in mankind as a whole. Each nation in turn realizes an aspect of God/Nature, so that 'God is the real hero of world history' (3:569).

These two tracks, the rational and the pantheist, must soon converge on a utopia which will satisfy both the spirit and the body. Man will be intellectually liberated. Even now, in Heine's opinion, man is mature enough no longer to need the tutelage of priests. Kant had defined Enlightenment as 'man's emergence from a state of immaturity that was due to his own deficiencies'.[17] Heine wants to go further. Not only, he says, is man dissatisfied with the ideals preached by Christianity; man has rejected all abstract aims in favour of solidly material goals. Above all, man wants physical health. 'Our first task is to become healthy; for our limbs still feel very weak. The holy vampires of the Middle Ages have sucked out so much of our life-blood' (3:568). But not only must man be cured: matter must be redeemed from the scorn that Spiritualism has cast upon it. 'The first object of all our new institutions is the rehabilitation of matter' (3:568). And the pantheist utopia is described in a famous passage of *History*:

> Happier and more beautiful generations, conceived in freely chosen embraces, who grow up in a religion of joy, will smile sorrowfully at their poor ancestors, who gloomily abstained from all the pleasures of this fair earth, and, by deadening their warm and colourful senses, were reduced almost to chilly spectres. Yes, I say it with certainty, our descendants will be happier and more beautiful than we. For I believe in progress, I believe that mankind is destined to be happy, and thus I think more highly of divinity than those pious people who think mankind was created only to suffer. Here on earth, by the blessings of free political and industrial institutions, I should like to establish that bliss which, in the opinion of the pious, will come only in heaven, on the day of judgement (3:518-19).

Heine spelled out his programme in less exalted terms in a letter to Heinrich Laube. Following Saint-Simon's doctrine, he pointed out that modern industrial and economic resources made it possible to produce and distribute enough goods to provide not only the necessities of life but also luxuries for everyone. A religion that promised happiness only after death was now superfluous. 'People will take our meaning when we tell them that in future they will eat beef instead of potatoes every day and work less and dance more. Depend upon it, people are not asses' (10.7.1833).[18]

But Heine also develops the religious aspect of the Saint-Simonian vision. Man's religious needs will be satisfied on this earth, but religion will no longer be a separate part of life. Instead of being confined to one day out of seven, spirituality will be set free to pervade the whole of life, and the everyday world will be transfigured. The clearest indication of what Heine means by this comes in his articles on *French Painters*, where he describes a painting, 'The Reapers', by the now forgotten artist Léopold Robert. Heine notes that Robert has been compared to Raphael, but adds that while Raphael spiritualizes earthly beauty, turning it into something ethereal, Robert brings out the solid materiality of his harvesters, wagon and cornfield, and yet the figures also seem like timeless inhabitants of a transfigured and holy earth: 'they know no sin, their daily task is an act of worship, they pray continually without moving their lips, they are blessed without a heaven, redeemed without a sacrifice, pure without constant cleansing, completely holy' (3:56).

Although Heine writes as an advocate of Sensualism, what he proposes is a dialectical synthesis of Sensualism and Spiritualism. The result is one of the many compelling utopian visions produced by the nineteenth century. One thinks of the free society that Goethe's Faust envisages just before his death, or of Walt Whitman's celebrations of democracy. The French Revolution had at least swept away an oppressive social order and held out the prospect of a radical transformation of human life. And the enormous expansion of industry and technology was transforming the physical conditions of life with unheard-of rapidity. It was not unreasonable to hope that the industrial power unleashed by capitalism could be harnessed and used to establish a just and free society.

If the twentieth century has often seen such hopes severely disappointed, a reason for their frequent failure can be gathered from Heine's essay. He insists that the final victory over Spiritualism will not occur in the realm of ideas. It will be real, practical, material. It will take the form of a German revolution, in which the religious energy of Germanic pantheism will be allied to the intellectual blast-power of post-Kantian philosophy. We saw above that Sensualism, completely unspiritualized, took gross and brutish forms. And Heine admits that the full arsenal of

Sensualism contains some ugly weapons. It will reanimate the savage fighting spirit of the ancient Germans, which Christianity fortunately tamed but did not extinguish. But now that Christianity itself is almost extinct, 'the old stone gods will arise from the forgotten rubble, and Thor with his gigantic hammer will at last leap to his feet and smash the Gothic cathedrals' (3:639). One might fancy that Heine's prophetic vision had carried him forward to the 1930s.

In this passage, the conclusion to *History*, there is no pleasure or triumph, only grim foreboding at the prospect of the German revolution. Nor does Heine suggest that the revolution will lead straight to utopia, though many commentators have put these words in his mouth. There is simply a lacuna in his forecast of the future. The lacuna results from the hesitation in Heine's own thought, mentioned earlier, between unqualified Sensualism, in which man resigns all claim to a spiritual nature, and the reconciliation of Sensualism with Spiritualism, of the body with the spirit. Heine wants both alternatives: the former as a means, the latter as an end. He wants to mobilize the liberating energies of the senses, including their gross and cruel elements, for a final struggle against the oppressive power of the spirit. But in any society worth inhabiting, sensuality has to be controlled and civilized, and for that it must enter into a synthesis with reflection and self-discipline. If Spiritualism has been destroyed, how can these aspects of it help in the construction of an ideal society? How can the revolutionary means avoid defeating the utopian end? The revolution envisaged by Heine looks likely to prove as self-destructive as the French Revolution did in Hegel's analysis. In the next chapter we shall see Heine, in the years before 1848, becoming increasingly certain that an actual revolution would take place in Europe, and increasingly pessimistic about its outcome.

3

BETWEEN REVOLUTIONS

Heine and his generation reached maturity in the political doldrums between the Congress of Vienna of 1815, which restored stability to Europe after the defeat of Napoleon, and the revolutions of 1848. Of the preceding generation, Wordsworth had lived in France soon after the Revolution of 1789, which he passionately supported; of the next generation, Baudelaire fought on the Paris barricades in 1848. Heine, a more political poet than either, had almost no opportunity for active involvement in politics, but remained an observer. His political attitude moved from early enthusiasm for emancipation, and excitement over the revolution of July 1830 in France, to disillusionment with the middle-class society that flourished under the July Monarchy, and thence to a painfully ambivalent foreboding of proletarian revolution. His journalistic writings, in particular, are full of reflections on the various political systems known to him in Germany, France and Britain, as well as those he knew by report in Russia and America. His comments on these systems show him searching for the complex truth concealed behind official manifestos.

Heine felt himself to be living at the end of a heroic age of politics. It had begun on 14 July 1789 with the fall of the Bastille, symbolizing the defeat of feudal authority by popular revolt, and with the Declaration of the Rights of Man and of the Citizen issued by the French National Assembly the following month. The first article of the Declaration ran: 'Men are born and live free and equal under the laws. Social distinctions can be founded only on the general good.'[1] This seemed to Heine as epoch-making an event as the rise of Christianity. Freedom, he announces in 1828, is the new religion of our age, and Christ is one of its high priests. 'But the French are the chosen people of this new religion, the first gospels and dogmas are written in their language, Paris is the new Jerusalem, and the Rhine is the frontier that separates the consecrated land of freedom from the land of the Philistines' (2:601).

Unlike Hegel, Heine was not dismayed by the execution of Louis XVI and the Reign of Terror. He admitted that the surgical operations performed by Danton and Robespierre on French society had required excessive use of the guillotine. But at least it was a quick death: 'the patient was not tormented for long, not tortured or broken on the wheel, as many thousands of *roturiers* and *vilains*, townspeople and peasants, were tortured and broken in the good old days' (2:600). Modern historians estimate that the Terror claimed 17,000 official victims in fourteen months, while the number of avoidable deaths from starvation and disease under the old regime must have been far greater.[2] Heine would probably have agreed with the more recent judgement that 'to dwell on the horrors of revolutionary violence while forgetting that of "normal" times is merely partisan hypocrisy.'[3]

The fall and execution of Robespierre in July 1794 led to more moderate government under the Directory of five elected members, which governed France from 1795 to 1799. It was overthrown by Napoleon, who made himself First Consul and later Emperor. Although this might seem a defeat for freedom and equality, Heine saw Napoleon as continuing the Revolution by embodying its ideals firmly in institutions. For example, Napoleon had established the French code of civil law and given French public life a firm meritocratic structure, which it still retains.

However, Heine gives less attention to Napoleon's achievements than to his myth. Napoleon's defeat of the old-established European powers made him a modern hero. And his ill-fated Russian campaign, from which only one-sixth of his 610,000 troops returned, was an appropriately heroic downfall. In 1828 Heine wrote of Napoleon: 'his name already sounds as ancient and heroic as the names Alexander and Caesar' (2:593). He read with fascination the accounts of Napoleon's life on St Helena that appeared soon after the exile's death in 1821. He particularly admired Count Ségur's *History of Napoleon and the Grand Army in 1812* (1824). 'This book is an ocean,' he wrote to his friend Moses Moser, 'an Odyssey and Iliad, an Ossianic elegy, a folk-song, a sigh from the heart of the French people!' (Oct. 1825). Ségur's narrative seemed to him to resemble Homeric epic in its grand sweep, its celebration of war, and in recounting the downfall of a hero comparable to the Achilles of the *Iliad* or the Siegfried of Germanic legend; and its account of the burning of Moscow reminded him of the fire in which the heroes of the *Nibelungenlied* perish.

A liberal like Heine could subscribe to the cult of Napoleon, because it was a popular cult. In France, Heine found that ordinary people still regarded him as a godlike figure: an old soldier begged Heine for a sou 'in Napoleon's name' (3:120). And Heine claims that in the London docks he communicated with some Indian seamen by saying: 'Mahomet!' to which they replied, beaming: 'Bonaparte!' (2:594).

Heine gives literary form to the Napoleon myth in one of the most intricately constructed of the *Pictures of Travel*, the Sternean *Ideas: The Book of Le Grand*. Here Heine recounts how, as a child, he himself saw Napoleon, when the latter visited Düsseldorf in 1811. Heine's description opens with the word 'Hosanna!' so that Napoleon's ride through the Hofgarten in Düsseldorf becomes a parody of Christ's entry into Jerusalem. Later Heine speaks extravagantly of Napoleon's martyrdom at the hands of the British, and forecasts that his grave on St Helena will become a Holy Sepulchre to which future generations will make pilgrimages. But Napoleon is also represented in this book by a French drum-major, Monsieur Le Grand, who, since he can only speak French, instructs the child Heine by beating out the history of the Revolution and Napoleon's campaigns on his drum. Heine then tells how, on revisiting his home town long afterwards, he again meets Le Grand, who is ragged and ill, having returned from Russia. Le Grand once more drums the history of Napoleon, but this time his drumming ends in a dead march which evokes the fate of the Grand Army outside Moscow.

Napoleon's defeat and banishment were followed by the

restoration of the Bourbon monarchy in France, while the rest of Europe was dominated by the Holy Alliance of Prussia, Russia and Austria, all determined to suppress any revolutionary stirrings. Heine did not easily reconcile himself to living in such an unheroic age, especially after the paeans to emancipation he had uttered in the *Pictures of Travel*. He was justifiably excited by the revolution in France in July 1830. After three days of street fighting, provoked by the government's suspension of press freedom, the Bourbon king Charles X fled to England, and the Duke of Orléans, whose father had been a member of the revolutionary National Assembly, was proclaimed the citizen-king Louis-Philippe. This revolution heartened liberals through-out Europe: it installed a king responsive to his subjects' wishes; and, compared to the French Revolution, it seemed bloodless, though in fact some eight hundred of the insurrectionaries were killed and four thousand wounded.[4] Heine, some years later, recalled and stylized his feelings in the *Letters from Heligoland* which form the second section of his polemic *Ludwig Börne: A Memorial* (1840). When news of the Revolution reached him during his holiday on Heligoland, it seemed to inaugurate rule by the people. A fisherman who takes Heine out in his boat sums up the news in the words: 'The poor people have won!' (4:54). Heine thus implies that the poor understand the essential meaning of political events. He hopes that the revolution will spread throughout the world: to Spain and Siberia, to Naples and Ireland, where 'Paddy may make a bull that will wipe the smile off the English face' (4:58); perhaps even to Germany.

Such hopes were bound to be disappointed by the prosaic reality of the July Revolution, which ushered in the rule of the French bourgeoisie. It offered a *juste milieu* (happy medium) between reactionary royalism and radical republicanism. Though a constitutional monarchy governed by the Chamber of Deputies, it was scarcely a democracy by modern standards. France had only one elector for every 170 inhabitants, while Britain after 1832 had one per 25.[5] Significantly, its first prime ministers, Laffitte and Périer, were bankers. Its outstanding politician, the historian Guizot, urged his countrymen: 'Strengthen your institutions, become enlightened, become rich, improve France's moral and material situation.'[6] He justified the restricted franchise as encouraging hard work and frugality. This was in keeping with the regime's *laissez-faire* economics, which benefited financiers. 'It was not the French bourgeoisie that ruled under Louis-Philippe,' wrote Marx in 1850, 'but one section of it: bankers, stock-exchange kings, railway kings, owners of coal and iron mines and forests, a part of the landed proprietors associated with them—the so-called finance aristocracy. It sat on the throne, it dictated laws in the Chambers, it distributed public offices, from cabinet portfolios to tobacco bureau posts.'[7] The regime, however, also imposed tariffs to protect French manufacturers against international competition, and forbade the organization of trade unions. Balzac called the *juste milieu* 'an insurance contract drawn up between the rich against the poor'.[8] And Heine, as early as 1832, describes a typical 'juste-millionaire' who, on noticing a man dying of hunger in the streets, explains this away as a piece of anti-government propaganda (3:151).

In 1831–2 Heine sent to Germany a series of reports on French politics and culture, later collected under the title *Conditions in France*, in which we can see him coming to terms with the unheroic modern world. Paris gave him his first experience of constitutional and parliamentary government, and he used his journalism to examine its strengths and weaknesses, contrasting it with the reactionary or radical alternatives offered by its opponents and with the revolutionary struggles from which it had incongruously emerged.

Heine soon decided that, despite its grandeur, the age of heroes like Robespierre would have been too strenuous to live in. 'I cherish the memory of the earlier revolutionary struggles and the heroes who fought them ... but yet I should not like to live under the rule of such sublime beings, I could not stand being guillotined every day' (3:207). He also revised his opinion of Napoleon. Napoleon should have been Europe's George Washington (3:65), but he betrayed the cause of freedom by allowing himself to be anointed Emperor. He too belonged to the past. His statue on the Place Vendôme was imposing and inhuman, a monument to a basically self-seeking heroism which the present, Heine hoped, would no longer require. A hero of a more suitable type was Lafayette, who had drafted the Declaration of the Rights of Man and of the Citizen, but had also tried to protect the French royal family against popular hatred. In July 1830 he commanded the national guard which helped to instal Louis-Philippe. Thanks to his steady and lifelong support for liberty, Lafayette was loved by the people as a fellow-human, not deified like Napoleon. He embodied the ideals of the present—freedom along with peace and security: 'They revere him as a kind of Providence on horseback... as a spirit of freedom who also ensures that there is no pilfering in the fight for freedom' (3:121).

In the present peaceful, constitutional age, violent revolution too might be a thing of the past. Perhaps, after the Bourbon interlude, the July Revolution had attained the essential aims of 1789. Both republicans and royalists in post-1830 France, were, in Heine's opinion, 'plagiarists of the past' (3:126), still peddling obsolete ideas. Advocates of the *ancien régime* were mere ghosts, while republicans were trying to transplant the ideas of Robespierre to an unpropitious climate.

Heine criticized both, but he was especially bitter about the aristocratic and clerical groups which wanted to restore the Bourbons. The hostility to aristocracy which runs through his writing is most pungently stated in *Kahldorf on the Nobility* (1831), a pseudonymous book by a liberal journalist, to which Heine contributed a preface. The book itself is a very mild critique of the aristocracy. It suggests that they occupy too many high administrative posts, but also praises them for providing a model of cultivation and dignity. Heine's preface is very different, in both tone and substance. He declares that, in an age that aspires to liberty and equality, the aristocracy is obsolete. Why should aristocrats expect privileges in return 'for having taken the trouble to be born' (2:661)? At present, he complains, the European nobility virtually monopolizes high military and diplomatic posts and thus forms an international league to enforce the repressive policies of the Holy Alliance. Under the old regime, the French aristocracy had brought revolution upon itself by keeping the people in a politically benighted state. The loyalty their successors professed to Louis-Philippe is simply a hypocritical pretence. The citizen-king looks for support to the people, not to the untrustworthy and self-seeking aristocracy: hence Heine's admiration for 'the idea of a citizen-king without court etiquette, without page-boys, without courtesans, without procurers, without diamonds dispensed as tips, and such-like splendour' (2:665). In the very first sentence of *Conditions in France* Heine notes with satisfaction the abolition of the hereditary peerage in France, and comments: 'The hereditary peers have made their last speeches' (3:106). The final two words, in English, equate the peers with British criminals whose last speeches, delivered from the scaffold, were copied down and sold as broadsheets.

Heine was particularly hostile to the German aristocrats. Napoleon's reorganization of Germany in 1803 and 1806 had abolished over two hundred petty principalities. Though the princes retained only their titles, they still expected deference, and, worse still, they received it. Heine is appropriately sardonic about 'this smiling without saying anything, saying without thinking anything, and all these aristocratic skills which make the good citizen gape as though they were marvels of the deep; but any French dancing-master performs them better than the German nobleman, who had them laboriously drummed into him in bear-licking Lutetia [i.e. Paris], and who, at home, transmits them to his descendants with German thoroughness and heavy-handedness' (2:231). Besides expressing class antagonism, Heine is making an acute sociological point here: earlier in European history the aristocracy did advance civilization by cultivating manners; but now anyone can hire a master to teach him these skills, and so the aristocracy is culturally, as well as politically, obsolete.

The republicans Heine encountered in Paris seemed as great a danger to constitutional government as the reactionaries were. He found a large colony of German political exiles, dominated by Ludwig Börne; and he also met French republicans at meetings of the radical Society of the People's Friends. These groups, unlike the Saint-Simonians, did not propose to replace the present social hierarchy with a hierarchy of innate talent, but demanded radical equality. Although Heine suspected that the

pleasure-loving character of the French would make it difficult
for them to relinquish the attractions of monarchy, liberal
society seemed to have an inbuilt tendency towards levelling-
down and egalitarianism. By exposing all authority to challenge,
it favoured mediocrity. In addition, Heine considered the French
to be naturally irreverent and unwilling to acknowledge any
authority, whether political or intellectual. Their national
character, together with their social system, might lead ultimate-
ly to an egalitarian republic as envisaged by Robespierre. Heine
imagined such a republic as resembling ancient Sparta, which he
calls 'that great tedious patriotism-factory, that barracks of
republican virtue' (3:116).

In order to ward off reaction and republicanism, Heine was a
convinced advocate of constitutional monarchy. For this he had
two main reasons. One was that without monarchy life would
be intolerably dull and grey, and that monarchy preserves the
traditions of the past. Reporting on the Paris Salon of 1831, he
writes at length about the painting by Delaroche which shows
Cromwell gazing down at the dead Charles I, as coolly, in
Heine's view, as a woodcutter might look at a fallen oak (3:67).
The execution of Charles I in 1649 was for Heine a great
symbolic moment. The Stuart monarchy still retained the poetic
aura derived from medieval chivalry and the splendour of
Catholic ceremonial. By contrast, Cromwell was tough, unimaginative, indifferent to the emotional and aesthetic claims of
tradition. He and his Puritans had destroyed 'merry England'
(which Heine had heard about in A. W. Schlegel's lectures) and
spread a gloomy piety over their country like a grey fog (4:174).
Heine, as we shall see, thought that Cromwell's spirit persisted in
the commercial and utilitarian England of his own day.
Similarly, according to Heine, modern republicans take a blindly
utilitarian attitude to monarchy, and want to abolish it because it
serves no obvious function. Heine calls such people 'icy-clever
political thinkers, sober Bacchantes of reason, who in their
logical frenzy would like to argue away from the depths of our
hearts all the awe that the ancient sacrament of kingship
commands' (3:63). He illustrates this point with the story (surely

much too good to be true) of an Englishman who disturbed his contemplation of Delaroche's picture by remarking to him, in a croaking voice: 'Do you not think, Sir, that the guillotine is a great improvement?' (3:67). This character had so entirely lost his reverence for kings that he was interested only in the most efficient technique for beheading them.

Heine's second argument is that a monarch can represent the interests of the people against the intermediate social strata, especially the aristocracy, who want to exploit them. Hence a monarch must be a citizen-king, directly accessible to the people. As early as the *Letters from Berlin* Heine had praised the modest demeanour of the King of Prussia, who rode through the streets of Berlin in an ordinary carriage, dressed like any other army officer, and was admired for his genuine qualities as soldier and family man (2:14). Heine thought he had discovered a similar ruler in Louis-Philippe, though the latter's occasional interventions in politics made Heine suspicious that he might be plotting to gain absolute power. However, Heine defended Louis-Philippe against his detractors. Caricaturists loved to depict the portly Louis-Philippe as a giant pear, to mock his felt hat and his umbrella, and to deride his practice of shaking hands with his subjects, which formed a potentially comic contrast with the hauteur of the Bourbons. In retrospect, these look like the symbols of ordinariness expected of a modern democratic politician, and Heine was perceptive in seeing Louis-Philippe's hand-shaking as a form of political ritual appropriate to modern society: 'the manly handshake may become a symbol of the new civic monarchy, as servile kneeling became the symbol of feudal sovereignty' (3:279).

However, there are two obvious contradictions in Heine's monarchism. Firstly, if monarchy is supposed to preserve colour and tradition in modern society, then it fails to do that by becoming constitutional, popular, and dispensing with august ceremonial. British history shows that it has been necessary to invent new traditions to support the symbolic role of the monarchy.[9] Secondly, the constitutional limitations on a monarch's power must debar him from effectually acting on behalf of his people. In a long discussion of constitutional monarchy, Heine defends the principle that 'the king reigns, but does not govern' (3:183-4), which assigns the monarch a purely symbolic role.

These contradictions may explain why Heine at other times speaks favourably of absolutism. He had been impressed by Napoleon's summary treatment of the German princes. In *Journey from Munich to Genoa* (1828), while Heine is crossing the battlefield of Marengo and thinking about the autocrat Napoleon, his travelling companion, a German from the Baltic region of Russia, asks him: 'Are you a good Russian?' and thus puts him in mind of another autocrat—the Tsar. At this time Russia, with support from Britain and France, was helping the Greeks in their struggle for independence from Turkish rule. Heine's reply, 'Yes, I am a good Russian' (2:379), comes after long reflection on the paradox that the absolute monarchy of Russia is assisting emancipation more actively than the parliamentary democracy of Britain. The reason he gives is that Britain is firmly in the grip of a reactionary aristocracy, while in Russia a succession of autocrats has reduced the power of the church and made the aristocracy not a self-serving feudal caste, as in other countries, but a body enrolled in the service of the state. Hence the defence of freedom has passed to Russia.

Heine was misled into thinking Russia a defender of freedom by his friend, the Russian poet and diplomat Feodor Tyutchev, whom he got to know in Munich in 1828. Although the nobles had indeed been turned, notably by Peter the Great, into a hierarchy of state servants, it was absurd to see an ally in Tsar Nicholas I, who ruled a police state under the slogan 'Orthodoxy, Autocracy, Nationality'. In 1831 Russian troops brutally suppressed the Polish uprising; as Heine put it, the Russian wolf had disguised itself as a kindly grandmother, only to gobble up the Red Riding Hood of freedom. In the same year Heine declares that autocracy can never be compatible with constitutional freedom: not Russia but France now represents the way forward (2:665). We may find more prescience in his later description of Russia as 'that terrible giant, who is still asleep and growing in his sleep, with his legs stretching into the fragrant gardens of the East and his head knocking against the

North Pole, dreaming of a new world empire' (4:79).

However, Heine's dalliance with autocracy is not a complete deviation from his beliefs. In his private notebook he returns to the subject, comparing the Russian autocracy with the dictatorship exercised by the National Convention at the height of the French Revolution (6:634). A passage in his essay on Shakespeare even equates autocracy and democracy. Discussing *Julius Caesar*, he says: 'The best democracy will always be the one in which a single man, as the incarnation of the people's will, governs the state as God governs the world' (4:201). Hence he interprets Caesar as an admired autocrat like Napoleon, while the conspirators are motivated both by aristocratic selfishness and by mean republican hatred for an outstanding individual. This aspect of Heine's political thinking, which one critic has called 'constitutional Caesarism',[10] is difficult to square with his liberalism; but it needs to be understood in relation to his aversion to levelling-down and his increasing insight into the political effects of the July Monarchy's *laissez-faire* economy.

Although Heine hoped that constitutional monarchy would safeguard France against both reaction and republicanism, he was uncertain whether it could withstand the power of finance. *Conditions in France* includes a memorable description of the Bourse, the Paris Stock Exchange, full of images of mechanical coldness. The international financial system was at the furthest remove from the heroic ideal of politics which Heine was reluctantly discarding. If Périer was a giant among modern statesmen, then the speculators of the Bourse, in Heine's opinion, are dwarfs; he also anticipates modern Zürich by calling them gnomes (3:192). Périer's death was not marked by the slightest variation in the rate of exchange. The Bourse is indifferent to the destiny and aspirations of mankind. It is a political thermometer, responding only to variations in the stability of Europe. Its speculators react to events like the fall of Warsaw with the same automatic instinct that makes frogs croak when rain is approaching. 'Not "to be or not to be", but stability or instability, is the great question at the Bourse' (3:194).

The inhuman imagery which Heine applies to the Bourse

links it with his comments on Britain, where he spent four
months in the summer of 1827. He stayed mostly in London,
with excursions to the seaside at Margate and Ramsgate, and
since he could read English but not understand it when spoken,
he had few social contacts. But he saw all the sights, visiting the
House of Commons, the Old Bailey, Drury Lane Theatre,
Bedlam and (it appears) a brothel in Regent Street. London
seemed to him the utmost development of commercial society,
and he seems to have felt somewhat as a present-day British
visitor may feel in New York. In 'English Fragments', another of
the *Pictures of Travel*, he again casts himself as a dreamy poet, and
describes how, as he lingers at the corner of Cheapside to gaze at
a picture in a shop-window, the hurrying crowds elbow him
aside with exclamations of 'God damn!' (2:539). The picture he
is contemplating shows Napoleon crossing the Beresina—the
heroic antithesis to this soulless modern society. However, Heine
also dwells on how attractively goods are displayed in the
London shops: even a plateful of raw fish is laid out with as much
artistic skill as a Dutch genre painting (2:541). But he notices,
too, the crossing-sweepers who (like Jo in Dickens's *Bleak House*)
made their living by sweeping away mud and horse-dung. His
description of the London streets anticipates Walter Benjamin in
singling out the features of modern urban experience: the
anonymous crowds, the incongruous juxtapositions (Napoleon/
Cheapside), and the magical aura surrounding saleable com-
modities.[11]

Heine's comments on the English people are sometimes
intensely hostile. He denounces their church-going, their
money-grubbing, and the profound tedium he imagines at the
heart of their lives. His powers of caricature were further
stimulated by encountering British visitors to the Continent.
These, the pioneers of modern tourism, remain prosaically
unmoved by all they see: 'The scent of the lotus does not
intoxicate them, any more than the flames of Vesuvius warm
them. They drag their tea-kettles to the latter's very rim; and
there they drink tea spiced with cant' (5:305). Britain had
developed machine civilization to such a pitch that its people had
become automata:

Yes, wood, iron and brass seem there to have taken possession of the human spirit and to have been driven almost crazy by it; while the dis-spirited human being, like a hollow ghost, performs its accustomed tasks in a mechanical manner, and at the appointed time devours beefsteaks, delivers parliamentary speeches, cleans its fingernails, climbs into the stage-coach, or hangs itself (1:589).

Heine was puzzled by British politics. Britain had brought about the first modern revolution; the execution of Charles I was a more epoch-making event than that of Louis XVI. But it had led only to Puritanism and commercialism, while the British aristocracy had survived by making itself inconspicuous and was now securely in power. Before the passing of the 1832 Reform Bill, Heine was scornful about it. Yet Heine admitted that Britain had produced a heroic statesman in the liberal George Canning, 'the Spartacus of Downing Street' (3:145), and a valuable political journalist in William Cobbett, whose attack on the British national debt Heine partially translated into German. And he was impressed by the extent to which the Opposition could resist the government, and by the firmness with which British politicians had withstood Tory attempts to stifle the Reform Bill.

Although Heine never visited America, he imagined it as resembling Britain without Britain's redeeming features. In the 1820s, admittedly, he spoke enthusiastically about Washington and American liberty. After the Prussian decree of 1822 excluding Jews from the public service, he and his friend Eduard Gans even contemplated founding a Jewish settlement in North America; Heine referred to it ironically as 'Ganstown' (letter to Moses Moser, May 1823). But travellers' reports persuaded him that America had adopted the ruthless commercialism and the hypocritical piety of England, and that its democracy was in practice the rule of the rabble. It was 'that Freedom Stable where / All the boors live equally' (D 633; 6:101). Dickens, who did visit America and had his liberal hopes disillusioned, describes it similarly in *American Notes* (1842). Heine was also aware that both freedom and equality were limited. They were denied to several million blacks, and even in the North, where slavery had been abolished, racism persisted. Heine tells how the daughter of a New York clergyman married a black man, whereupon, in Heine's English, 'She was flinshed' (4:39)—i.e. lynched. Heine thought that in a classless society mob rule must prevail, for no one would have the authority to restrain the mob or to inculcate higher standards of civilization. America, in fact, struck him as the furthest imaginable extreme from the heroic past; and at times he feared that it typified the future. The prophecy made by Napoleon on St Helena, that before very long the world would be either an American republic or a Russian empire, would come true. 'What a prospect!' Heine wrote. 'The best we can hope for is to die of monotonous tedium as republicans! Our poor grandchildren!' (5:286).

Such forebodings are frequent in *Lutetia*, the reports from Paris which Heine wrote in the early 1840s for the *Augsburg Gazette*. They reveal his disillusionment with the July Monarchy and the increasingly radical views which were soon to be encouraged by his friendship with Marx. After describing the entombment of Napoleon's remains in Paris in 1841, Heine wrote: 'The Emperor is dead. With him died the last hero of ancient mettle, and the new world of Philistines breaths a sigh of relief, as though released from a brilliant nightmare. Above his grave rises an industrial bourgeois age which admires quite other heroes, such as the virtuous Lafayette, or James Watt the cotton spinner' (5:341). The bourgeois age was dominated by manipulation and mediocrity. Louis-Philippe now seemed a skilful hypocrite, combining the duplicity inherited from his ancestors with the cunning of a modern politician (5:241–2). The old charisma of royalty had now passed to the financier Baron Rothschild: 'Even outside the door of his office many people shiver with awe, like Moses on Mount Horeb,' Heine noted. 'Money is the god of our age, and Rothschild is its prophet' (5:355).

Heine thought that industrial expansion and railway speculation had bred in the French middle classes a money-grubbing spirit such as he had previously associated with Britain, and he allows himself much sarcasm at the expense of the bourgeoisie. Reporting on the uninspiring Salon of 1843, he surmised that the mediocre paintings reflected the mercenary narrowness of the age. Thus in a picture of the scourging of Christ, 'the central figure, with his expression of suffering, looks like the chairman of a bankrupt company, who has to appear before his share-holders and render accounts' (5:481). The reign of the bourgeoisie set limits to freedom. For example, private owner-ship made the daily press not a democracy but an oligarchy, and limited freedom of expression with a strictness that the German censorship could not match. As a rule, only wealthy industrialists or financiers could afford to found a newspaper; to ensure large sales they aligned it with a political party; and any article that failed to conform to the paper's political line, or was deemed of insufficient general interest, would be rejected (5:281–2). Heine's account of the press may be set beside the detailed analysis of the publishing industry given at the same time by Balzac in *Lost Illusions* (1837–43); and it has an obvious relevance to the present.

Heine acknowledged that Guizot, the virtual head of the government from 1840 to 1848, was a politician of principle. He respected the work which Guizot, as minister of education, had previously done to strengthen the middle-class regime by spreading education among the people—a contrast to the behaviour of the aristocracy of the *ancien régime*, who had brought revolution upon themselves by keeping the people ignorant. Heine too thought that the people were not yet ready for sovereignty. They must not only be fed, but also washed, civilized and educated. At present they were more likely to follow demagogues who flattered them than pedagogues who offered to instruct them. But Guizot, besides being hampered by his schoolmasterly manner, had little time left to accomplish his task. Heine thought he was like a man trying to bring in the harvest under the shadow of an approaching thunderstorm, while most people had not even noticed that the sky was darkening (5:461).

What was this thunderstorm? In 1843 Heine remarked that if he had lived at the time of the Emperor Nero, as Rome correspondent for a provincial newspaper, his colleagues would have mocked him for neglecting court festivities and intrigues in order to report the activities of an obscure sect of Galileans (5:496). Yet these Galileans had conquered the Roman Empire, and Heine thought it would not be long before the proletariat seized power in France and Britain. 'Although Communism as yet is not much talked about, and sprawls on its miserable pallet in obscure garrets,' he warned in 1842, 'this is the sombre hero who is destined to play a great though transitory part in the modern tragedy, and is only waiting for his cue to come on stage' (5:405).

Throughout Europe, the 1840s were the 'bleak years' of crop failures and economic recession. Nothing on the Continent, admittedly, rivalled the Irish famine of 1846–7, which killed a million people and drove another million to emigrate, but the potato blight also deprived the lower classes of northern France and Germany of their staple diet. Eastern Germany saw the first of several bad grain harvests in 1845. In 1847 there were bread riots in Berlin. France too had bad harvests, which sharply increased the cost of basic foodstuffs: between 1845 and 1847 the price of bread in Paris rose by fifty per cent. At the same time an industrial crisis produced unemployment and wage reductions. Nationally, the number of people helped by public assistance rose from 835,000 in 1845 to 1,186,000 in 1847. In the industrial town of Lille, with 76,000 inhabitants, 29,000 were receiving public assistance.[12] In some rural areas, masked men threatened to kill landowners who sent grain to the towns; bands of beggars roamed the countryside, bakeries were plundered.

Revolution was widely feared, especially in Britain, where the Chartist movement held vast public meetings (sometimes with audiences of 200,000) to demand the vote for all male adults. In 1842, after the suppression of strikes and riots in much of England, Heine foretold that Chartism would produce a social upheaval that would make the French Revolution look tame, because it would attack the sanctity of private property (5:421–2). Similarly, Engels in 1844 maintained: 'Social strife is gradually developing into combat between two great opposing camps—the middle classes and the proletariat', and expressed surprise that 'the bourgeoisie should remain so complacent and placid in the face of the thunderclouds which are gathering overhead'.[13] Ironically, Britain was almost the only country in Europe that was not affected by revolution in 1848.

A foretaste of revolution in Germany came in 1844. The Silesian weavers, whose cottage industry could not compete with the mechanized textile manufactures of Britain, had been reduced to such misery that we hear of starving families clad in rags and glad to eat the flesh of dead horses.[14] Their insurrection of 1844, quickly suppressed by troops, inspired Heine's bitter poem 'The Silesian Weavers', with its prophetic warning to Germany:

> 'The shuttle flies, the loom creaks loud,
> Night and day we weave your shroud—
> Old Germany, at your shroud we sit,
> We're weaving a threefold curse on it,
>   We're weaving, we're weaving!' (D 544; 4:455)

This poem was itself partly based on a song sung during the uprising of the Lyons silk-weavers in 1831, which threatens: 'We shall weave the old world's shroud' (4:971). Heine's poem in turn passed into popular currency, for we hear of it being distributed as a broadsheet in Berlin.

The keynote of *Lutetia* is set by the fourth article, dated 30 April 1840. Here Heine recounts a visit to the Faubourg Saint-Marceau, an industrial suburb of Paris, to find out what the workers were reading. He found the spirit of 1793 being revived by editions of Robespierre's speeches, while Communism was being propagated by such recent publications as Etienne Cabet's *People's History of the French Revolution* and '*Babeuf's Doctrines and Conspiracy*, by Buonarroti' (5:251). The work of Cabet, who claimed the support of the New Testament for his utopian community of equal workers, but who abjured all revolutionary and violent methods, need not detain us. But Babeuf and Buonarroti deserve more attention.

François-Noël ('Gracchus') Babeuf was a revolutionary extremist who in 1796 led a conspiracy against the Directory. It was discovered, and Babeuf was guillotined. He was a thorough-going egalitarian. The Manifesto of Equals, drawn up by one of his associates, denounces the formal equality guaranteed by the Revolution as insufficient. It demands that equality should be realized in the lives of citizens. 'Equality must not only be recorded in the Declaration of the Rights of Man and of the Citizen; we want it in our midst, under the roofs of our houses,' it proclaims. 'Let there be no distinctions among people other than those of age and sex. Since all have the same needs and the same capacities, let them all have the same education and the same food.'[15] In a sentence that even Babeuf thought too dangerous to publish, all superfluous luxuries are dismissed, including the arts: 'Let the arts perish, if need be, so long as we retain true equality.'[16] Buonarroti, another of the conspirators, published his account of Babouvian doctrines in 1828. His book influenced extreme radicals in the 1830s. Of these, the most prominent was Louis-Auguste Blanqui, who adopted Babeuf's conspiratorial methods when forming his secret society, the Society of the Seasons, in 1837. A revolutionary movement, Blanqui believed, must be led by a dedicated vanguard which would seize power by force and rule on behalf of the workers; the phrase 'dictatorship of the proletariat' originates with him. Blanqui's attempt to seize power in May 1839 was crushed within hours, but it gave substance to Heine's fears that popular discontent would breed revolution.

When Heine speaks of Communism, he usually means the ascetic, egalitarian Communism of Babeuf. He also agrees with the utopian socialism of Cabet in ascribing Communist ideals to Jesus. Heine quotes the 'saying of the divine Communist' that it is easier for a camel to pass through the eye of a needle than for a rich man to enter the kingdom of heaven (5:453).

Babeuf's egalitarian Communism was severely criticized by Marx in the *Economic and Philosophical Manuscripts* of 1844. Marx complains that it takes no account of goods which cannot be shared because they are not material, such as artistic talent. Being based on the same acquisitiveness and envy as capitalism, it envisages only a levelling down, an 'abstract negation of the whole world of culture and civilization, a regression to the unnatural simplicity of the poor man without any needs'.[17] The Communism advocated by Marx, on the other hand, was intended to conserve the achievements of civilization and make them freely available to all who wanted them.

Marx wrote this in Paris, where he arrived in October 1843, after the political review he edited had been suppressed by the Prussian government. Heine met him that December, and became a close friend of the Marx family. Both published in the same radical German émigré journals. Heine's 'The Silesian Weavers' and two satirical attacks on King Friedrich Wilhelm IV of Prussia appeared in *Forwards* (*Vorwärts*), as did an essay in which Marx, inspired by the Silesian uprising, foretold a social revolution in Germany. This provoked the Prussian government to pressure the French into suppressing *Forwards* and deporting Marx, early in January 1845, to Belgium. Marx and Heine remained in touch, and saw each other briefly in 1848 and 1849, shortly before Marx settled in London.

Heine described Marx as 'the most determined and the most intelligent' of the German refugees in Paris (5:466), and critics, especially in East Germany, have readily assumed that Heine adopted Marx's radicalism. But Nigel Reeves has shown that the influence went the other way. Marx's own early poems reveal the influence of the *Book of Songs*, and his fragmentary novel, *Scorpion and Felix*, that of the *Pictures of Travel*. More importantly, Heine's acerbic satires on people like Börne were the model for such Marxian polemics as *The Great Men of Exile* (1852). And Marx was also indebted to Heine's political interpretation of German philosophy. Heine inspired even the famous statement of 1844, 'Religion is the sigh of the oppressed creature, the feeling of a heartless world, and the soul of soulless circumstances. It is the opium of the people'.[18] This seems to have been suggested by Heine's description of Christianity, in 1840, as a delusory palliative for man's actual infirmities: 'All honour to a religion which eased the suffering of mankind by pouring into the bitter cup some sweet tranquillizing drops, spiritual opium, a few drops of faith, hope and charity!' (4:111). And Heine in turn may have been induced to connect religion with opium by contemporary Paris caricatures in which the British, forcing the Chinese to buy opium, are represented as missionaries entering China with Bibles in their hands and opium dealers at their back.

Although Marx's analysis of capital, labour power and alienation leaves no trace in Heine's writings, he does seem to have persuaded Heine that Communism need not take the form of Babouvist egalitarianism. Heine continued to imagine the workers seizing control of the apparatus of industry and using it to ensure their material well-being, in accordance with Saint-Simonian expectations. In a discussion of Communism in 1844 he quotes the doctrine of hedonism which he had put forward ten years earlier in *History*, and warns that the people are no longer constrained by the morality associated with Christianity. They want a heaven on earth such as Heine describes in the opening section of *Germany: A Winter's Tale*, written after his return from a visit to Germany—his first for twelve years—in the autumn of 1843:

> Why shouldn't we be happy on earth,
> why should we still go short?
> Why should the idle belly consume
> what working hands have wrought?
>
> There's bread enough grows here on earth
> to feed mankind with ease,
> and roses and myrtles, beauty and joy,
> and (in the season) peas.
>
> Yes, fresh green peas for everyone
> as soon as the pods have burst.
> Heaven we'll leave to the angels, and
> the sparrows, who had it first. (4:578)[19]

In December 1844 Engels published in a radical London newspaper, *The New Moral World*, an article headed 'Rapid Progress of Communism in Germany'. He included a translation of 'The Silesian Weavers' and claimed that Heine, the greatest German poet, 'has joined our ranks'.[20] But this was another instance of Engels's notorious optimism. Earlier that year, Heine had written a poem, 'Voyage of Life', expressing misgivings about his rapprochement with the German radicals (4:420). And he seems to be alluding to Marx when he writes, in 1854:

> The leaders of the German Communists, operating largely underground, are great logicians, and the acutest have emerged from the Hegelian school and are undoubtedly the ablest men and most resolute characters in Germany. These revolutionary theologians and their ruthlessly determined pupils are the only living political forces in Germany, and it is to them, I fear, that the future belongs (6/ii: 186–7).

Misgivings are evident even in *Germany: A Winter's Tale*. It includes a sinister sequence in which the poet, wandering at night through the streets of Cologne, finds himself accompanied by a figure carrying an axe. This is the executioner whose deeds turn the poet's thoughts into action, as Heine had warned in *History*: 'Remember this, you proud men of action. You are merely unconscious agents of the men of ideas' (3:593). There follows a dream in which the poet, with his companion, again passes through the streets, but this time he has a gaping wound in his chest, and he marks the doorposts with blood from his own heart. Each time he does so, a faint death-knell is heard.[21] Finally they reach the Cathedral and enter the Chapel of the Three Kings (i.e. the three wise men from the East who visited the infant Jesus). The executioner pitilessly smashes these relics of the past, and a stream of blood bursts from the poet's own heart just before he wakes. The implication is clear: monarchy and religion belong to the dead past, but so does the poet. His ironic role is to proclaim the revolution in which he will be among the first victims.

Sometimes Heine goes further and describes Communists as an appalling threat. In 1842 he warns that they will swarm forth like rats from the ruins of present society (5:414). By 1855 they have become 'demons lurking in the lower strata of society' (5:238), 'the most terrible crocodiles ever to arise from the slime'

(5:239). Such passages recall the contemporary notion that Paris, where immigration from the country had increased the population from some 714,000 in 1817 to over a million by 1846, was inhabited by 'dangerous classes', a vast, swarming underworld of vagrants and criminals, ready to exploit any political disturbance as a pretext for mayhem. Thus Thiers, in a speech of 1850, denounced 'this mob of vagabonds with no avowed family and no known domicile' as the chief danger to political stability.[22] However, Heine is usually more perceptive: he notes in 1840 that it is the skilled workers among whom the writings of Robespierre, Cabet and Buonarroti are circulating (5:251), and was proved right by the fact that those arrested for taking part in the insurrection of June 1848 were predominantly craftsmen and shopkeepers. It seems clear that skilled workers, not the unemployed or criminals, were the revolutionary vanguard.[23]

Heine's perceptions were sometimes distorted by his fastidiousness, which could amount to snobbery. In his *Confessions* he says that he would wash his hand if the sovereign people were to touch it (6:468). He disliked tobacco-smoke and did not enjoy the society of working-class revolutionaries. Once in Hamburg, Heine tells us, he was introduced to the ex-tailor Wilhelm Weitling, who greeted him warmly as a fellow-revolutionary. Heine felt embarrassed and ashamed to find himself in such company, especially as Weitling not only kept his cap on and remained seated in Heine's presence, but also kept rubbing his leg; he had been chained up in various prisons, he explained, and his leg still itched where the iron ring had chafed it. Heine, as he reports his feelings, was disgusted that a man who had been in prison should address him with such vulgar familiarity. He was not afraid of being caught in Weitling's company, but rather of being hanged in such company (6:470). In all this account there is not one word of sympathy for Weitling, whose political sufferings far exceeded anything Heine had undergone.

Heine, then, did not care for the working classes, and he generally imagined their revolution as introducing a republican equality far more severe than Robespierre's. In a private notebook, Heine imagines Parnassus being levelled and covered with tarmac to make a highway or a railway. Another notebook entry runs: 'Democratic rage against love-poetry—why sing the rose, aristocrat! sing the democratic potato that feeds the people!' (6:653). But though he disliked this prospect, he was too honest to dismiss the people's claims, like the liberal Tocqueville, as an 'obscure and erroneous notion of right' serving 'envious and greedy desires'.[24] For many years Heine himself had been repeating the saying of the French revolutionary Saint-Just: 'Bread is the people's first right' (3:23, 3:570, 4:200).

The resulting ambivalence gives rise to some of the best of Heine's later writing. Two instances, one in verse and one in prose, may be singled out. The poem 'The Roving Rats' begins by reducing society, under a thin disguise, to the kind of blunt opposition that Marx and Engels favoured:

> There are two kinds of rat:
> One hungry, and one fat.
> The fat ones stay content at home,
> But hungry ones go out and roam. (D 783; 6:306)

This antithesis, however, long antedates Heine's acquaintance with Marx. As he pointed out, he had drawn attention to 'the great soup question' (1:340) in his early tragedy *William Ratcliff* (1823), where thieves in a London tavern discuss the division of society 'into two parties, waging furious war: into the full and the hungry' (1:353). The later poem describes the unstoppable onset of the starving proletarian rats who care nothing for religion, morality, or even for 'property, the palladium of the moral state' (6:307—a dig at Hegel). Their attackers will listen only to 'reasoning based on roast beef or fish, / With sausage citations to garnish the dish' (D 784). A terrible prospect, but in Heine's allegory the propertied classes are rats as well, preparing to fight ruthlessly to retain their privileges.

Perhaps the most famous statement of Heine's ambivalence occurs in the preface to the 1855 French edition of *Lutetia*, where he recalls his earlier remark that the Communists could afford to wait, because the future was theirs. The disquiet with which he made this prophecy, he now says, was by no means feigned. A Communist world will have no place for art. The laurel groves will be chopped down and potatoes planted; the lilies of the field will be set to work spinning; and the *Book of Songs* will be made into paper bags to hold coffee or snuff for the old women of the future. But an inner voice, Heine goes on, tells him with compelling logic that since he cannot deny the premise, 'All men must eat', he must accept the consequence—Communism (5:232–3).[25]

For a Communist revolution Heine foresaw two possible outcomes. Sometimes he imagined that the revolution could only be short-lived, because its egalitarianism would deprive it of the services of outstanding personalities, entrust power to 'the tanner and the sausage-seller' (5:252), and thus prove self-destructive. But another outcome was conceivable in which a successful revolution would spread all over the world. The word 'Weltrevolution' (world revolution) appears to have been coined by Heine (5:406). This would allow short-sighted egalitarianism to destroy the achievements of civilization. At worst, it would combine tyranny with equality:

> Perhaps there will then be only one shepherd and one flock, a free shepherd with an iron crook and a human flock all shorn equally and all bleating in unison! The rumblings of a dark, sombre age are approaching, and a prophet writing a new Apocalypse would have to invent new beasts, such terrible ones that St John's old animal symbols would be only mild doves and amoretti in comparison. The gods hide their faces in compassion for humankind, their charges for so long, and perhaps also in concern for their own fate. The future smells of Russian leather, blood, godlessness and many beatings. I advise our grandchildren to be born with extremely thick skin on their backs (5:406–7).

Heine wrote this in 1842. Six years later, revolutions broke out all over Europe: in Vienna, Berlin, Budapest, Naples and Milan. The revolutionary impulse came from Paris, where a campaign for extension of the franchise developed into popular demonstrations and then, after clashes with troops, into open insurrection on 24 February. Louis-Philippe panicked, abdicated and fled to Britain. A Provisional Government was set up which gave all adult men the vote and set up national workshops for the unemployed. The April elections, however, returned a moderate majority which decided on a showdown with Socialism and proceeded to dissolve the workshops. This provoked the insurrection of 23–26 June in which fifty thousand workers took up arms. Some fifteen hundred were killed and nearly twelve thousand arrested. The political uncertainty that followed helped Louis Napoleon, a nephew of the Emperor, to enter the political limelight. In December 1848 he was elected President of France, with a majority of nearly four million votes over his closest rival; three years later he carried out a *coup d'état* and proclaimed himself Emperor. Marx, following events from Britain, commented that the tragic events of the first French Revolution were now being repeated as farce, with the nephew in place of the uncle.[26]

Heine had little attention to spare for these events, for by now he was terminally ill. In 1848 a long history of ill health culminated in his physical collapse, and for the remaining eight years of his life he was to be bedridden. On the second day of the February insurrection, on his way to a hospital, Heine got caught up in the street fighting; his carriage was overturned and used to build a barricade. He managed to write three short, rather superficial articles for the *Augsburg Gazette* on the events of February, but the margin of the second has a note to the editor: 'Dear Kolb, I can no longer see, and cannot walk two steps. Your poor friend H. Heine' (5:212). During the June days he was staying in Passy, a Paris suburb. Though remote from the fighting, he imagined it vividly, and the bloodshed apparently helped to drive him back to believing in God. Soon afterwards he wrote to his Hamburg publisher, Campe: 'This is universal anarchy, the world turned upside down, divine madness become visible! The Old Man will have to be locked up if things go on like this. It's the fault of the atheists for irritating him into a frenzy' (9.7.1848). In 1850 he spoke of the June days to a visitor: 'The cannons' thunder assailed my ears. I heard the shrieks of the dying; I saw Death mowing

74

down the young men of Paris with his terrible scythe. At such hideous moments pantheism is not enough; you have to believe in a personal God, in an existence beyond the grave' (W 2:155). But Heine's route back to God was a more circuitous one than this account acknowledges, and it will be traced in the next chapter.

4

BETWEEN RELIGIONS

The complexities of Heine's attitude to Judaism and Jewishness can be illustrated from a letter he wrote to his close friend and fellow-Jew Moses Moser on 23 August 1823. Heine describes how he has just revisited Hamburg, where he had many relatives (including his uncle Salomon Heine, a millionaire banker), and how 'the magic of the place' has stirred his emotions. 'If I were a German,' he continues '—and I am not a German, see Rühs and Fries *passim*—then I would write you long letters and great emotional narratives on this subject.' He goes on to mention the individuals he has met in Hamburg; some he likes, some he dislikes; then comes the generalization: 'The Jews there are miserable scoundrels; if one wants to take an interest in them, one has to avert one's eyes; and I find it more agreeable to keep my distance from them.' He has, however, attended a service conducted by Isaak Bernays at the orthodox synagogue; and though he considers Bernays a 'charlatan', he has more respect for him than for the proponents of Reform Judaism in Hamburg and Berlin. His own acquaintances in Hamburg believed that he was attached to Judaism, but he has dispelled this illusion: 'I confess that I shall enthusiastically support the rights of the Jews and their civic equality, and in bad times, which must come, the Germanic mob will hear my voice resounding in German tap-rooms and palaces. But the born enemy of all positive religions will never champion that religion which first intro- duced the fault-finding with human beings that now causes us so much pain; and if I nevertheless do it after a fashion, there are special reasons: tender emotions, obstinacy, and care to maintain an antidote.'

At first sight, this letter seems a mass of contradictions. But if we unpack its contents, item by item, we shall find that Heine is

giving honest expression to the ambivalences that a German Jew
was liable to feel in an age of partial liberalization.

Let us begin with Heine's attitude to Judaism as a religion. He
recalls in his *Memoirs*: 'I was born at the end of the sceptical
eighteenth century and in a town which during my childhood
was ruled not only by the French but also by the French spirit'
(6:557). Düsseldorf was occupied by French forces from 1795 to
1801, and was again under French rule from 1806 until the fall of
Napoleon. In 1815 it was incorporated into Prussia, but retained
the Napoleonic Code, including the civil rights of Jews; Jews
elsewhere in Prussia had received comparable rights only in
1812. Even before the French occupation Heine's parents had
come under the influence of the Enlightenment and wanted to
become assimilated to Gentile society. Heine tells us that his
mother's religion was 'strict deism, wholly in keeping with her
prevailing rationalism' (6:562); she was an admirer of
Rousseau's *Emile* and brought her children up in accordance
with Rousseau's precepts (e.g. feeding them herself instead of
employing a wet-nurse). His father was slower to assimilate,
judging from his membership of certain Jewish mutual aid
associations; but he later became a Freemason, which an
orthodox Jew could not have done. Although they may have
continued to celebrate Passover by the traditional *seder* meal,
Heine's parents seem to have had little interest in Judaism. Heine
was sent to a Hebrew school in early childhood, but did not
learn much there. In adult life he displays scanty knowledge of
Hebrew and makes gross errors in traditional knowledge: thus in
a letter to his publisher Campe he corrects his previous statement
that the destruction of Jerusalem occurred on the tenth of Ab
instead of the ninth (7.9.1851). From the age of six until sixteen
he attended Catholic schools and appears not to have suffered
any anti-Semitic hostility.

When Heine accuses Judaism of encouraging 'fault-finding
with human beings' (*Menschenmäkeley*), he is quoting from one
of the masterpieces of the German Enlightenment, Lessing's
philo-Semitic play *Nathan the Wise* (1779). The accusation is
uttered by a bigoted Christian character and is answered by the

tolerance, wisdom and readiness to forgive his enemies shown by Lessing's hero Nathan. By this quotation Heine asserts his allegiance to the international humanism of the Enlightenment, and endorses the Enlightenment critique of traditional Judaism. To the Enlighteners, orthodox Judaism seemed mainly concerned with ritual and superstition, typified by the famous dispute between the scholar Jacob Emden of Altona and the chief rabbi of Hamburg, Jonathan Eybeschütz, about the amulets containing Kabbalistic formulae which the latter sold to pregnant women as a safeguard against puerperal fever. Such superstition was equally opposed by Lessing's friend Moses Mendelssohn, the great Jewish philosopher of the Enlightenment. He wanted to discard it and lay bare the essence of Judaism. While Christianity required its adherents to accept its central dogmas on faith, the essential content of Judaism was law founded on reason. 'All [Jewish] laws,' Mendelssohn asserted, 'refer to or are founded on eternal truths of reason, or recall them to mind and arouse one to the contemplation of them; so that our rabbis are right to say that the laws and teachings are related to one another as body is to soul.'[1] So when Heine rejects Judaism along with other positive religions, it is the orthodox Judaism of Bernays that he has especially in mind. Elsewhere he shows his admiration for Mendelssohn by a comparison with Luther: Mendelssohn has liberated the Jews from the authority of the Talmud, as Luther threw off the authority of the Pope (3 : 583).

But why in that case does Heine object to Reform Judaism? Here Heine is responding to a difficulty created by Mendelssohn. In his anxiety to show that Judaism contained nothing incompatible with reason, Mendelssohn left open the question what was then distinctive about Judaism. He himself wore a beard, followed the dietary laws, and would not write or travel on the Sabbath. Such an attachment to tradition is understandable, but is it rational? Why need the rational soul remain housed in a Jewish body? Mendelssohn's children fell away from Judaism; most spectacularly, his daughter Dorothea married Friedrich Schlegel and was converted to Catholicism along with her husband. Mendelssohn's pupil David Friedländer drew an obvious conclusion by arguing that since Judaism consisted of basic religious truths available to all mankind, the Jews should discard any distinct identity. The proponents of the Reform movement thought it necessary to adapt, not the theology of Judaism, but its mode of worship, to make it more acceptable in Protestant North Germany. Services were shortened; parts, including the sermon, were conducted in German; passages were sung by a choir, accompanied by an organ. Heine would have none of this. He described Friedländer and his ilk as corn-cutters who were trying to cure Judaism of a skin-disease by blood-letting, and thus making it bleed to death (to Wohlwill, 1.4.1823).

It would seem, then, that Heine wanted not to deny but to affirm his Jewish identity. But this is hardly compatible with his intemperate outburst against the Hamburg Jews as 'miserable scoundrels'. While Heine had many Jewish friends, his image of the Jews as a people was an unflattering one, and he apparently shared some of the 'antipathy to the Jews' that he attributed to his mother (letter to Betty Heine, 7.5.1853). He certainly agreed with a central tenet of Enlightenment philo-Semitism: to be admitted to European society, the Jews must abandon their distinctive appearance and customs. Thus Mendelssohn insisted that Jews must give up Yiddish and speak standard German. The Prussian administrator C. W. Dohm wrote, at Mendelssohn's request, a book arguing that the present 'corruption' of the Jews resulted from oppression and would vanish once they were given civil rights. And Heine praised another Berlin philo-Semite for trying to 'help poor Ikey, who is trodden underfoot like a worm, to climb on to the bench of humanity' (letter to E. C. A. Keller, 1.9.1822).

By 'corruption', the Jews' well-wishers meant their enforced concentration on commerce. Heine sometimes identifies the Jews outright with commerce. Thus a letter to his Gentile friend Christian Sethe, written when Heine was eighteen, calls Hamburg a 'huckster town' and adds 'I call everyone in Hamburg a Jew' (27.10.1816). When he wrote this letter, Heine was working as an apprentice in the banking house owned by his Uncle Salomon, who later set him up in business as 'Harry Heine & Co.' As a businessman Heine was an unmitigated failure, and presently his family saw that there was nothing for it but to send him to university. His letter reveals his frustration at being forced into an uncongenial profession; but it also shows the seeds of the attitude fully developed in Marx's notorious essay 'On the Jewish Question' (1843): 'What is the secular cult of the Jew? Huckstering. What is his secular god? Money.'[2] Since the association of Jews with the lower forms of commerce was so strong, we find Heine in the early 1820s casting around for a different and more acceptable Jewish identity.

This was forced on Heine also by the growth of German nationalism, with its attendant anti-Semitism. Rühs and Fries, mentioned in his letter, were nationalist academics who published pamphlets violently attacking the Jews. Rühs was prepared to tolerate Jews who converted to Christianity and completely abandoned Jewish ways; Fries was less conciliatory: 'Judaism is a residue from the uncultured past, which instead of being restricted should be completely extirpated. In fact, improving the condition of the Jews in society means rooting out Judaism, destroying the whole lot of deceitful, second-hand peddlars and hawkers.'[3] In the summer of 1819 famine and industrial depression provoked anti-Semitic riots throughout Germany, in which mobs burnt synagogues and looted houses and shops belonging to Jews; these were known as the 'Hep-Hep' riots because of the rioters' war-cry. They provoked a wave of conversions to Christianity, including that of Moses Mendelssohn's eldest son Abraham (father of the composer). Thus the 'Germanic mobs' Heine mentions are not metaphorical. By locating them in 'palaces' as well as tap-rooms, Heine is referring to the anti-Jewish legislation enacted in Prussia during the 1820s. In 1822 the Prussian government declared Jews ineligible for university posts; subsequent decrees debarred them from various high professional and social positions.

All this hurt Heine badly, for he was inclined to identify closely with the Germans. On 7 March 1824 he described himself to Christiani as 'one of the most German beasts in existence', and continued: 'I love everything that is German more than anything else in the world, it is a joy to me, and my breast is an archive of German feeling, just as my two books are an archive of German song.' But here, as in *The Harz Journey*, Heine shows his ironic ambivalence by crediting the German character with emotional depth but also with the pedantry that files all experiences away in an archive. Two months earlier he had written to Moser: '"May my right hand wither, if I forget thee, Yerusholayim"—these are the words of the Psalmist, more or less, and they are still mine' (9.1.1824). Ambivalence here is evident from Heine's vagueness about the quotation and from his use of the Hebrew form of the name 'Jerusalem' as pronounced by German and Polish Jews. While evoking the deepest Jewish nostalgia, he simultaneously mocks himself by his anachronistic use of dialect.

If Heine was to be compelled to adopt a Jewish identity, and if no acceptable Jewish identity existed, then one had to be constructed. He had a glimpse of a different form of Jewishness in 1822, when he briefly visited the part of Poland that was under Prussian rule. His essay *On Poland* (1823) describes the Polish Jews, including his impressions of a *shtetl*:

The external appearance of the Polish Jew is horrible... But disgust soon gave way to compassion when I examined the condition of these people more closely and saw the holes, resembling pig-sties, in which they live, talk Yiddish, pray, huckster and—are wretched (2:76).

Besides feeling compassion, Heine decides that the Polish Jew, as yet untouched by Western influences, is a more authentic being than the Western Jew who puts on Western clothes, fills his head with Western ideas, yet fails to become properly European. His demand for cultural integrity shows him applying to the Jews the Romantic conception of the homogeneous *Volk*. In doing so, he anticipates the conception of the Eastern Jew as the authentic Jew which was to be put forward almost a century later by Martin Buber and Arnold Zweig.[4]

For Heine, however, authentic Jewishness lay not in the East but in the past. When he wrote the above-quoted letter to Moser, both of them were members of the Society for Jewish Culture and Scholarship (*Verein für Cultur und Wissenschaft der*

Juden) which had been founded in Berlin in 1821. Other active members included the legal historian Eduard Gans, a friend (and frequent satirical target) of Heine's, and the philologist Leopold Zunz. Zunz had studied classical philology at Berlin under F. A. Wolf, who pioneered the textual study of Homer, and August Böckh, one of the founders of modern hermeneutics. Wolf and Böckh studied the Greek and Latin classics by critically examining their text and reconstructing their historical context as a means of interpreting them. Zunz wanted to apply these methods to the Old Testament and other records of Jewish history. Thus, while Friedländer was willing to discard Judaism altogether, Zunz and the other members of the Verein were remote from traditional Judaism in their daily lives, but wanted to regain contact with it through the scholarly reconstruction of the past.

Heine joined the Society on 4 August 1822 and took part in its activities until he left Berlin in May 1823. The Society was not large: it had some fifty members in Berlin, and another twenty in its Hamburg branch. It conducted a school to prepare Jewish boys, many of them from Poland, for admission to educational institutions in Berlin; Heine taught French, German and German history in this school for three hours a week, and was apparently an inspiring teacher. But by May 1823 the Society was beginning to disintegrate. The journal in which its members published scholarly articles ran only to three issues. The Society was finally suspended in February 1824. Afterwards Heine wrote to Moser that *Kuggel* (a Sabbath dish baked with honey, sugar and noodles) 'has done more to preserve Jewishness than all three numbers of the Journal. And it has found a lot more takers' (14.12.1825). In 1844 he wrote an essay in memory of one of the Society's members, Ludwig Marcus, who had recently died insane. Heine describes the members of the Society with affection and respect. But he regrets that their learning was merely antiquarian, not living and organic. 'Intellectually gifted and generous-hearted men tried to rescue a cause that had long since been lost, and all they managed to find on the battlefields of the past were the bones of the ancient warriors' (5:179).

Philology, then, did not give access to the Jewish past. But the Romantic interest in national history had brought forth another means of reconstructing the past: the historical novel, pioneered by one of Heine's favourite writers, Walter Scott. Soon after the suspension of the Society, in the summer of 1824, Heine set to work on a Jewish historical novel, *The Rabbi of Bacharach*. It was a way of making contact with the living spirit of Judaism, not the dead letter transcribed in the Society's Journal. And it promised to satisfy the emotions that stirred Heine as he delved into Jewish history. During his studies he wrote to Moser: 'The spirit of Jewish history reveals itself to me more and more' (25.6.1824). Two poems on the Jewish past, 'To Edom' and 'Burst out in loud lamenting' (1:271), eloquently convey his feelings. Unfortunately, his more ambitious project was soon put aside. He returned to it in 1840, but the new portion sits uneasily with the old, and the novel was never completed. The incongruities in the text, however, are due less to the history of its composition than to Heine's ambivalence about Jews and Judaism.

A leisurely introduction sets *The Rabbi* in the late Middle Ages, and in a series of anti-Semitic persecutions which began with the Crusades and were to culminate in the expulsion of the Jews from Spain in 1492. It opens in Bacharach, a small town on the Rhine. Heine describes the celebration of Passover in loving detail which recalls the genre paintings of Moritz Oppenheim and Isidor Kaufmann.[5] Two strangers enter and are made welcome; but the Rabbi discovers that they have smuggled in a dead child, so that they may charge the Jews with ritual murder. He flees with his wife Sara to Frankfurt, where they enter the ghetto. At this point comes the break between two periods of composition and between two modes of representing the Jews. Sara, the Rabbi, and the community surrounding them at Bacharach are depicted affectionately, in a mode combining historical nostalgia with domestic realism. But the Frankfurt ghetto is full of grotesques—the timorous Nasenstern ('Stern of the Long Nose'), the clown Jäkel the Jester, and a crowd of gossiping women. It also includes a renegade Jew, Don Isaac Abarbanel, nephew of a great Spanish rabbi, who, despite his conversion to Catholicism, is drawn to revisit the ghetto by his love of Jewish cooking. We have already noted Heine's fondness for *Kuggel*, and later, in his *Hebrew Melodies*, he apostrophizes *Schalet* (a kind of stew) in a parody of Schiller's 'Ode to Joy' (see D653). In 1831 Heine sat for his portrait to Oppenheim, who treated him to Sabbath lunch with *Kuggel* and *Schalet* and remarked on how nostalgic Heine must feel (W 1:225).

Oppenheim's comment was barbed. For by then, and long before he created Don Isaac, Heine himself had converted to Protestantism. On 28 June 1825, the former Harry Heine was baptized Christian Johann Heinrich Heine. Two years earlier he had told Moser that nobody in his family objected to his conversion; he himself did not consider it important, even as a symbolic act; yet self-respect kept him from taking the plunge (27.9.1823). We should remember that the Prussian state offered Jewish converts a baptismal gift of ten ducats if they named the King as their godfather, and that such mercenary conversions were vulgarly known as 'instant bleaching'. But the civil disabilities imposed on Jews by the Prussian legislature gave Heine little choice. When he did convert, however, it was reluctantly and in considerable secrecy. There is a covert allusion to it at the end of *The Harz Journey*, where the narrator describes himself standing on a lofty rock on which a cross is planted, feeling giddy, and clinging to the cross for support. 'No one will think the worse of me for having done so in such an uncomfortable position,' he concludes (2:162). After learning that Gans had likewise converted, Heine wrote to Moser: 'I should be very sorry if my own baptism should appear to you in a favourable light [i.e. as a genuine acceptance of Christianity]. I assure you that if the laws had allowed me to steal silver spoons, I should not have been baptized' (14.12.1825). In 1827, when depressed, he told a relative: 'All *meshumodim* [apostates] should feel as I do' (W 1:149); and his famous remark, 'The certificate of baptism is the entry ticket to European culture' (6:622), implies that even after baptism Jews were only allowed to be spectators. The portrayal of Don Isaac suggests that fifteen years later Heine was still uncomfortable about having converted. Don Isaac occupies a precarious position between religions, very like Heine's own: 'Yes, I am a heathen, and dislike both the dried-up, joyless Hebrews and the dismal, self-tormenting Nazarenes. May Our Lady of Sidon, the holy Astarte, pardon me for kneeling down in prayer before the grief-stricken mother of the Crucified One' (1:498). Like Heine, Don Abarbanel supports the senses against the spirit; and his secret devotion to the pagan goddess Astarte anticipates Heine's invocation of the Venus of Milo, the symbol of Hellenism, as 'Our Lady of Milo' (6:184).

In any case, Heine's conversion solved nothing. He remained uncomfortable about his Jewishness, and preferred to say that he was of Jewish ancestry (W 1:226). Crescence-Eugénie Mirat ('Mathilde'), whom he first met in 1834, began living with in 1836, and married in 1840, did not know that he was a Jew (W 2:175). In 1835 he untruthfully claimed never to have set foot in a synagogue (5:19). He allegedly said in 1844: 'I am not a Jew and have never been one' (W 1:566); but this could simply mean that he had never been a practising Jew. Perhaps he summed up his position best by saying: 'It would be distasteful and mean if, as people say of me, I had ever been ashamed of being a Jew, but it would be equally ridiculous if I claimed to be one' (W 2:175).

Despite his ambivalent feelings, Heine stalwartly defended Jews in the Damascus blood libel affair. In 1840, after an old monk mysteriously disappeared from Damascus, the Jewish community there was accused of ritual murder and subjected to persecution. The French consul supported the libel because of the French government's political interests in Syria. In his articles for the *Augsburg Gazette*, Heine exposed the absurdity of the charges, publicized the brutality with which 'confessions' had been extorted from suspected Jews, and called for action by the French government. Eventually, thanks to an international delegation including the Anglo-Jewish philanthropist Moses Montefiore and the French Jewish lawyer Adolphe Crémieux, the surviving prisoners were released and the blood libel was officially declared to be false. When he wrote about the blood libel in *The Rabbi of Bacharach*, Heine had thought that such superstitions belonged to the Middle Ages. (He evidently did not know that as recently as 1670 a French Jew had been burned alive in Metz on a charge of ritual murder; nor that such accusations had been raised in Russia during his lifetime, the latest being in 1830.) 'Such phenomena are a misfortune,' he wrote, 'whose consequences are incalculable. Fanaticism is an infectious disease which spreads in the most diverse form and will finally attack all of us' (5:268).

Despite this warning, Heine continued to see the history of the Jews as a story of progressive emancipation. He was undecided only on whether the Jews' contribution to history had already been made or was still incomplete. Sometimes, following Hegel, he speaks of Judaism as superseded, 'a petrified piece of world history' (2:515), and of the Jews as a 'ghostly people' watching over their buried treasure, the Bible (6:652). But he defines their contribution to past and future history most fully in the discussion of *The Merchant of Venice* in his Shakespeare essay. Having demonstrated Shylock's moral superiority to the Venetian Christians, Heine observes, following Mendelssohn, that the morality of the Jews is abstract, consisting in obedience to law. But this, he continues, makes it characteristically modern. The Greeks and Romans were devoted to something concrete—the soil of their native country; in the Middle Ages a vassal was devoted to the person of his feudal superior; but the Jews' devotion to an abstract principle, extended by Jesus to all mankind, anticipates the rationalism of the Enlightenment and the enthusiasm for abstract principles—liberty, equality and fraternity—generated by the French Revolution. As the ideals of the French Revolution spread, therefore, the rest of mankind is now catching up with the Jews. Instead of being a historical fossil, the Jews are in the front line of progress. 'Yes,' Heine declares, 'the cosmopolitan spirit sprang from the soil of Judaea, and Christ, who was really a Jew, founded a propaganda organization for international brotherhood' (4:258).

Defining the Jews' contribution to history, Heine sometimes draws on Messianic imagery. In a notebook entry he asks: 'Is their mission completed? I think it will be when the secular saviour comes: industry, work, joy—The secular saviour will come by railway' (6:652). Heine was not alone in this secularizing reinterpretation of Messianism: the Communist

Moses Hess wrote that the 'end of days' foretold in Jewish Messianism would in fact come when the summit of human progress had been reached.[6] Heine expresses this idea most memorably in a legend which he ascribes to the (fictitious) 'Rabbi Manasse ben Naphtali of Cracow' (4:120). The legend tells how the Messiah is so enraged by the maltreatment of the Jews that his hands have to be bound with golden chains lest he should lose patience and come too soon to relieve his suffering people. This seems to allude to the prohibition on 'pressing for the end', i.e. presumptuously trying to accelerate the Messiah's arrival by fervent prayer;[7] but if so, Heine has characteristically varied the tradition by representing the Messiah as anxious to hasten his own coming. Heine concludes with an implicitly political reinterpretation of Messianism: 'O do not lose heart, beautiful Messiah, who wishes to redeem not only Israel, as the superstitious Jews imagine, but the whole of suffering mankind!' (4:121).

Heine never seriously doubted that the Jews would eventually be granted full civil rights and be absorbed into the brotherhood of man. The modern state, he thought, could not tolerate an unassimilated enclave, and would therefore emancipate the Jews so that they could participate fully in national life. He believed the anti-Semitism of his day to be no longer religious but economic, based on a false identification of Jews with capitalists. It would therefore disappear when economic equality was established; and, as we have seen, Heine thought this would be achieved by Communism. Although he noted the racialist element in German nationalism, he thought it unimportant: 'Our nationalists, so-called patriots, with nothing in their heads but race and thoroughbreds and such-like horse-dealers' notions, these medieval stragglers will soon encounter opponents who will put a terrible end to all their dreams of Germanic, Latin and Slavic nationhood' (5:185). As we know, Heine was wrong. The twentieth century has seen repeated examples of modern states placing ethnic homogeneity above economic interest, and expelling or exterminating entire ethnic groups. Heine's failure to anticipate any of this shows that, despite its shortcomings, the age he lived in was exceptionally tolerant and secure.

Given that Heine was born, as he says, at the end of the sceptical eighteenth century, one would expect him to treat the Christian religion with at least as much irony as he displays towards Judaism. And indeed he does. But the sceptical irony inherited from the Enlightenment is only one component in his attitude to religion. Romanticism gives him an inwardness with religion and a feeling that religion is necessary for a fully human life. As we have seen, he regarded Saint-Simonianism as a religion. Even without feeling religious faith in any conventional sense, he intuitively understands people's need for it.

Heine's richest treatment of Christianity is in *The Town of Lucca* (1831), one of the *Pictures of Travel*. Its Italian setting encourages a comparison between the narrator's nominal Protestantism and the Catholicism flourishing all round him. Early on, therefore, Heine makes a light-hearted but acute comparison between the demeanours of Catholic and Protestant clerics:

> The Catholic priest behaves rather like a salesman employed in a large business; the Church, the great company whose director is the Pope, gives him a specified post and a specified salary for it; he works sluggishly, as anyone does who is not working on his own account, has many colleagues, and can easily remain unobserved in the flurry of business. His only concern is for the credit of the company, and that it should stay in business, since if it were to go bankrupt he would lose his livelihood. The Protestant clergyman, on the other hand, is always self-employed, and conducts religious affairs on his own account. Unlike his Catholic fellow-trader, he does not conduct wholesale trade, but only retail trade; and as he must manage it all on his own, he cannot be slack, he has to advertise his articles of faith, and cry down his competitors' articles; like a real retailer, he stands in his booth, full of commercial envy against all the big companies, especially against the great house in Rome, which employs many thousands of book-keepers and delivery staff and has trading-posts all over the globe (2:486–7).

Hence, Heine concludes, 'a Catholic priest strolls along as though Heaven belonged to him; a Protestant clergyman, on the other hand, bustles about as though he had taken a lease of Heaven' (2:487).

This passage reveals Heine's Enlightenment heritage, but also shows him rendering that heritage more complex. We know that he had read the account of the rise of Christianity in the fifteenth chapter of Gibbon's *Decline and Fall of the Roman Empire* (1776–88). Gibbon begins by saying that many of his readers will think the truth of Christianity, and its divine origin, a sufficient explanation for its rapid spread. 'But as truth and reason seldom find so favourable a reception in the world, and as the wisdom of Providence frequently condescends to use the passions of the human heart and the general circumstances of mankind, as instruments to execute its purpose, we may still be permitted, though with becoming submission, to ask, not indeed what were the first, but what were the secondary causes of the rapid growth of the Christian church?'[8] Confining himself to the secondary causes—the intolerance of the early Christians, the appeal of their doctrine of immortality, etc.—Gibbon quietly allows these historical factors to crowd out the 'primary causes', so that the alleged truth of Christianity comes to seem completely irrelevant.

Heine's ironic translation of Christian practice into commercial terms achieves something similar. It implies that some at least of the differences between Christian denominations can best be explained sociologically, with no need to refer to theological differences. But his analysis is not only more drastic than Gibbon's; it is double-edged. To the extent that we accept his analysis, it generates a second and more devastating irony. For if religion can be adequately translated into commercial terms, then commerce must have permeated the modern world to an alarming degree. Heine asks elsewhere: 'Does present-day religion consist in God become money or money become God?' (3:472). Here, he is not inviting the reader to share a secure sense of superior enlightenment. His irony is not a comfortable resting-place, but rather a trampoline which propels the reader back into the search for a truly religious basis to life.

Pursuing this search, *The Town of Lucca* proceeds from the structure of religion to its substance. Its Italian setting helps Heine to draw his favourite contrast between the spirit and the senses. Thus the narrator, walking in a sunny landscape, meets an aged monk in a rough robe and torn sandals; and in Lucca itself he catches sight of another monk, plump and bald, leaning out of a window with a naked woman beside him. Describing a religious procession, the narrator reflects that the priests in it look ill. But it is not their religion that has enfeebled them; rather, they represent the inherent weakness of all humanity. And he goes on to contrast the Greek religion of joy with the dismal religion introduced by Christ, 'a pale, blood-stained Jew with a crown of thorns on his head' (2:492). The Greek religion of joy was viable only when people were well and happy; but most people's lives are full of illness and suffering. Unable to feel pain, the Greek gods could not sympathize with mankind; but Christ, by sharing in human suffering, has enabled countless people to find in Christianity a source of love and consolation.

Besides pondering the ambivalence of Christianity, Heine introduces two figures to embody opposed positions, as Thomas Mann does with the Jesuit Naphta and the liberal Settembrini in *The Magic Mountain*. Heine's antitheses are two women, the Italian Francesca and the Irishwoman Lady Mathilde. Francesca is fervently pious: we first see her kneeling in prayer before an image of the Virgin, and later she kisses a wonder-working cross, kept in the cathedral at Lucca, with passionate devotion. But we are told that she is just as passionate in love as she is in prayer. Lady Mathilde, on the other hand, is an Enlightenment freethinker who mocks religion even in the cathedral. But, though she is sexually as well as intellectually liberated, she is said to be less sensual by nature than Francesca. Sexuality for her is an amusing game, and so is religion. Neither can inspire intense feeling in her. Francesca by contrast is a complete person: 'In her thoughts, her feelings, there was a Catholic unity' (2:508); while in Mathilde we recognize a fractured, one-sided personality, cut off, for better and worse, from the well-springs of faith and love. Which, Heine implicitly asks, is it better to be? Intelligent and shallow, like Mathilde; or passionate and rather stupid, like Francesca?

In *The Town of Lucca* Heine also introduces the concept of cosmic irony, which is to figure with increasing prominence in his thought. He recalls how, as a child, he read *Don Quixote* without appreciating its irony. He did not realize that chivalric romances had addled Don Quixote's wits and misled him into mistaking windmills for giants and a travelling barber for a knight errant. Rather, he thought that all Don Quixote's humiliations were somehow necessary, instead of resulting from the Don's own folly. *The Town of Lucca* exploits this notion in at least two ways. The credulity of the child Heine may be compared to the child-like faith of people like Francesca. As an adult, Heine has attained the viewpoint of Sancho Panza and seen through the illusion of religion. But here again Heine's irony rebounds on the reader. He suggests that one cannot do without profound beliefs, even if, like Don Quixote's, they are delusions and lead to humiliation. In supporting the cause of freedom in a reactionary world, is he himself not tilting at windmills, exposing himself to misfortunes as unnecessary as Don Quixote's? Nevertheless, he decides that it is more honourable to fight quixotically for freedom than to accept the mundane disillusionment of a Sancho Panza.

Long before writing *The Town of Lucca*, however, Heine had acknowledged irony as a governing principle both in literature and in the cosmos. *Ideas: The Book of Le Grand* is composed on the Napoleonic principle that 'from the sublime to the ridiculous it is only a step' (2:282). In it Heine cites the authority of the greatest dramatists, who all used tragi-comedy to convey their ironic insight into the futility of the world. Aristophanes used comedy to attack human self-esteem; Goethe adapted a puppet-play to explore the limits of human achievement in *Faust*; and Shakespeare placed the most searing truths in the mouth of the Fool in *Lear*. All of them were simply copying the 'primal poet', God, author of a cosmic tragi-comedy. As tragedy and farce alternate on the stage of history, 'God sits gravely in his box, or calculates that this theatre cannot stay in business much longer, because one actor is paid too much and another too little, and all

of them act execrably' (2:283). Heine's divine playgoer is one of
the many beings, tyrannical or ironic or malicious, whom poets
have imagined to fill the gap left by the decline of religion. He
has counterparts in Blake's Nobodaddy, in the spirits who watch
the Napoleonic wars in Hardy's *The Dynasts*, and in 'whatever
brute and blackguard made the world' in Housman's *Last Poems*.

Somebody so attached to the notion of cosmic irony, and so
adept in the practice of literary irony, might sense the appeal of
religion but could hardly be expected to succumb to it. And yet
in 1848 rumours began circulating that Heine had returned to
religion. He was variously reported to have embraced Protestantism, Judaism, or even Catholicism. To all except the most
naïvely pious, the news sounded like an intellectual collapse.
What had happened?

Whatever his intellectual state, Heine had suffered a decisive
physical collapse. His health had never been robust: even in his
twenties he was constantly complaining about headaches. In
his late thirties he was afflicted by intermittent eye trouble,
migraines, and local paralysis. Visitors in 1847 were shocked
to find him emaciated, partially paralysed and almost unable
to see without holding open his right eyelid. The final collapse
occurred in May 1848, when he was fifty. For the last eight
years of his life he was bed-ridden, tormented by spinal
cramps, often blind, and dependent on morphine for relief
from pain. To save his withered body from irritation, he had
to lie on mattresses piled on the floor, which he called his
'mattress grave' (6:180). And yet his mind was unimpaired.
Though speech sometimes cost him effort, he spoke with the
same inventive wit as before.

What Heine's illness was cannot be known for certain, but it
is widely thought to have been a form of syphilis which affected
the central nervous system and particularly the spinal cord,
though it was unusual in not damaging his brain. Some may
choose to see cosmic irony in the apostle of the senses being
struck down by venereal disease. But it might be more just to see
Heine's advocacy of the senses as a compensation for constitutional ill health. Similarly, the twentieth century's great

spokesman for the body, Mikhail Bakhtin, was crippled by polio from his mid-twenties onwards.

It cannot be doubted that in some strange way his illness did bring Heine back to God. But the nature of his return is perplexing, and is not made much clearer by the *Confessions* he wrote in 1854. Here he recants his religion of the senses. He speaks with particular enmity of Hegel, as having persuaded him that he was divine; but he seems to be conflating Hegel's philosophy with the Saint-Simonian religion, under whose influence, not many years earlier, he had called man the redeemer of God (4:575). Now, he declares, his incurable illness has taught him that he is only a poor, sick, miserable human being. 'I am no longer a life-loving, rather stout Hellene who smiled condescendingly upon dismal Nazarenes,' he announced in 1849; 'now I am only a poor, mortally ill Jew, an emaciated image of misery, a wretched human being!' (5:109). Of his religion, he says in his *Confessions*:

> Strange! After spending my whole life whirling about on all the dance-floors of philosophy, abandoning myself to all the orgies of the mind, whoring with all possible philosophical systems and remaining unsatisfied, like Messalina after a night of debauchery—now I find myself adopting the same standpoint as Uncle Tom, that of the Bible, and I kneel down beside my black brother with the same devotion (6:480).[9]

This, if we took it at face value, would be an extraordinary act of intellectual contrition. Heine's recantation would outdo the conversions or reconversions to Catholicism for which he had ridiculed so many of the German Romantics in *The Romantic School*. But, whatever his protestations, it is inconceivable that Heine should have adopted a standpoint of naïve devotion. Indeed he seems to have enjoyed puzzling his visitors with his new-found piety. When urged not to die with the reputation of a renegade, Heine replied in a mock-religious chant: 'Where health ends, where money ends, where the human intellect ends, Christianity begins' (W 2:122). He told others that the healthy and the sick needed different religions, and that Christianity was an excellent religion for the sick (W 2:205). But he assured his publisher: 'I have not become a Bible-thumper', and added that his change was an intellectual one, enforced by 'great, sublime, awe-inspiring thoughts' (to Campe, 1.6.1850).

Heine's religion was home-made, not the property of any church or denomination, and not wholly discontinuous with the beliefs he had explored earlier. He had, after all, never professed atheism. Since he had called religion necessary to suffering humanity, it was consistent that Heine, undergoing terrible suffering, should turn to religion. A turn to Christianity, however, is ruled out by Heine's many attacks on the hypocrisy of Christian love. A drastic instance is in the poem 'Brides of Christ', where the ghosts of nuns who have broken their vows throng a church at night and implore Jesus to let them into Heaven:

> Jesus wept upon our sin,
> For in him all mercies dwell,
> And he said: 'Your souls be curst
> And forever damned to hell!' (D 589; 6:42)

Occasionally Heine links Protestantism and Judaism in a manner recalling his earlier comparison between Mendelssohn and Luther. Thus in his *Confessions* he says that he now values Protestantism chiefly because it restored the Hebrew Bible to circulation, and goes on to compare Judaism and Protestantism because of their moral strictness. An affinity to Judaism is implied when he speaks of his 'serious conversations with Jehovah at night' (W 2:112), and in a letter to his brother Maximilian (3.5.1849) he says: 'May the God of our fathers keep you.' However, his religion is not rational nor ethical, and it is completely undogmatic.

Heine's new view of God and the world finds expression in the many poems he wrote on his sick-bed. These were published in two collections, *Romancero* (1851) and *Poems of 1853 and 1854* (1854); there are also numerous poems from these years which were not published in Heine's lifetime. The late poems are among the greatest and strangest of Heine's works, and also the most difficult to discuss. They sound like a voice from beyond the grave. Indeed Heine often speaks, for example in the postscript to *Romancero*, as though he were already laid in 'a grave without repose': 'Long ago my measure was taken for a coffin, and also for an obituary notice, but I am dying so slowly that it is gradually becoming as tedious for me as for my friends' (6:180). As he lay awake at night, racked by pain, he imagined that the wild thoughts rioting in his brain were ghosts, revelling in the skull of a dead poet (6:203). The poems in which he recorded these thoughts are like almost nothing else in literature, unless perhaps the speeches on death from *Measure for Measure* and *Hamlet*, or the prison scenes in Büchner's *Danton's Death*. Heine expresses the agony of his slow dying. He compares himself to Job—'time licks my wound, as the dog licked Job's sores' (6:135) —and adopts the persona of Lazarus, conflating the beggar 'full of sores' in Luke 16 with the man whom Jesus raised from the dead in John 12. But he also echoes the great *topoi* of despair from Homer and Sophocles. He alludes to the statement Achilles makes to Odysseus in the underworld: 'I would rather be above ground still and labouring for some poor portionless man, than be lord over all the lifeless dead' (cf. 6:239, 350), and to the words of the chorus in *Oedipus at Colonus*:

> Not to be born surpasses thought and speech.
> The second best is to have seen the light
> And then to go back quickly whence we came.
> (cf. 6:189, 333)[10]

In their range of tones, from playfulness to savagery, these poems have no counterpart except, perhaps, in late poems by Yeats such as 'The Circus Animals' Desertion'. Heine pours out his feelings regardless of consistency. He appeals to God to shorten his sufferings—'You know that I have no talent for martyrdom' (6:332)—but also protests against the bitterness of dying (6:326). He complains of the snail-like passage of time (6:202). He hates the sunlit world outside which mocks his wretchedness (6:189). Some poems of savage hatred are directed against his relatives, who he thought had cheated him out of the inheritance which was due to him after his Uncle Salomon's death in 1844. In one he lists his ailments in loathsome detail and bequeaths them to his enemies (6:120). In another he ponders the terrible Jewish curse 'May his memory be forgotten' (6:324).

And yet these curses only make sense within a religious horizon. 'Thank God that I have a God again,' Heine wrote to Laube, 'so that in extreme pain I can allow myself to curse and blaspheme. The atheist is denied such solace' (7.2.1850). Sometimes Heine's protests are restrained, as when he rebukes God for wasting a first-rate humorist (6:332), or when, in the *Confessions*, he complains that the cosmic irony which 'the great author of the universe, the heavenly Aristophanes' has visited on the little earthly ironist, 'the German Aristophanes', is altogether too cutting, and that the joke has gone on too long (6:499). Sometimes, however, his attitude resembles that imagined by Wittgenstein: 'If I thought of God as another being like myself, outside myself, only infinitely more powerful, then I would regard it as my duty to defy him.'[11] Heine takes on God most unforgettably in the poem beginning:

> Drop those holy parables and
> Pietist hypotheses:
> Answer us these damning questions—
> No evasions, if you please. (D 709, 6:201)

These are the questions put in the Book of Job, which Heine says elsewhere must have been inserted in the Bible as a homeopathic cure for man's propensity to doubt God's goodness (5:190-1). Job complains: 'The earth is given into the hand of the wicked: he covereth the faces of the judges thereof; if not, where, and who is he?' (Job 9:24). Similarly, Heine demands why the wicked are allowed to triumph, while the good are tormented and crucified. Is God not really omnipotent after all? Or, the most terrible suspicion of all, is God perhaps responsible for this injustice? 'Ah, that would be vile indeed.'

> Thus we ask and keep on asking,
> Till a handful of cold clay
> Stops our mouths at last securely—
> But pray tell, is that an answer? (*ibid.*)

In the original Heine conveys the futility of these persistent questions by an imperfect rhyme (*Handvoll / Antwort*). And he adds to the shock of his questions by adopting a forceful, unadorned style which was new in German and finds no echo until the late poems of Brecht, almost a century later. When Heine showed this poem to Alfred Meissner, one of the visitors to his sick-room, Meissner exclaimed: 'You call that religious? I call it atheistic.' 'No, no, it is religious,' replied Heine, 'blasphemously religious' (W 2:351).

Heine's tussle with God occupies only a minority of the late poems. His wide interests, and his wit, are still unmistakable. From his mattress grave he sees the world with humour, sometimes with compassion, but often with mordant cynicism.

While Heine earlier interpreted history as dialectical progress towards revolution or utopia, he now sees it as a parade of futility. His vision of history is summed up in the narrative about a string of pearls which is inserted as though gratuitously into the long poem 'Jehuda ben Halevy'. After the battle of Arbela, Alexander the Great found the pearls in the tent of the defeated King Darius of Persia, and tucked them away, along with all his other booty, in his 'baggy Macedonian trousers' (6:141). He gave the pearls to the dancer Thais, who was famous for having wantonly set fire to the city of Persepolis. After her death from venereal disease, the pearls were auctioned off to an Egyptian priest and found their way to Cleopatra's dressing-table. Cleopatra crushed one of the pearls to powder in order to display her opulence by swallowing it in wine. The remaining pearls were taken, in the course of the Arab conquests, to Spain, where they were displayed by Muslim rulers at tournaments and by Christian rulers at autos-da-fé. In the nineteenth century Mendizábal, the Spanish prime minister, pawned them to help pay off the national debt, and they were worn at the Tuileries by the wife of the financier Rothschild. This transition from Alexander to the banker whom Heine elsewhere calls 'Rothschild the Great' (2:431) may look like a movement from a heroic past to a sordid present, like that in Kafka's story 'The New Advocate' in which the war-horse of Alexander the Great adapts to the modern world by becoming a lawyer. But Heine is showing that history has always been a sordid parade of looters, courtesans and bankers. He stresses history's triviality by showing Alexander's captains receiving presents of jewels with childish delight, and by mentioning Aristotle, Alexander's tutor, only as 'the world's rump-thumper' (D 665). The persecution of the Jews is mentioned only in passing: Christian monarchs enjoyed 'the smell of old Jews being roasted' (6:144). In this perspective, achievement and suffering are equally meaningless.

Elsewhere Heine portrays history, more pessimistically, as a series of conflicts in which the race is always to the swift and the battle to the strong. The Valkyries, hovering over a battlefield, proclaim that the worse man will win and be hailed as conqueror (6:20). The brutal suppression of the 1848 revolutions shows this happening in the present (6:116). Royal dignity goes down before naked force. Charles I, in hiding, rocks the child of a charcoal-burner in whom he recognizes his future executioner (6:25). In the moving ballad 'Battlefield near Hastings', King Harold is killed and England enslaved by William the Conqueror; two monks, unable to find Harold's corpse, appeal for help to his former lover, Edith of the Swan's Neck, and after searching a graphically described battlefield she identifies the king's corpse by the love-bites on the neck (6:21). Harold's death symbolizes the joint defeat of royalty, love and Sensualism, leaving passionate but futile lamentation as the only possible response.

Politics and society are portrayed with equal disenchantment. In 'King David' a despot dies contentedly because he knows his son will carry out his Machiavellian instructions (6:40). After 1848 the Germans return to their domestic idyll, disturbed only by the occasional crack—'perhaps a friend being shot' (6:116). The unfeeling complacency of the well-off is repeatedly pilloried. A procession of orphans moves the citizens of

Hamburg to trifling acts of charity; the saccharine refrain 'O the pretty orphan children!' acquires more bitterness in each stanza (6:223). The corpses of two lovers who have died of cold and starvation (another defeat for Sensualism) are examined by a doctor who coolly diagnoses insufficient nourishment, and a deficient supply of warm blankets, as the cause of death (6:305). Most savage of all is 'The Slave Ship'. A slave-trader, afraid that his cargo will die on the Atlantic crossing, forces them into a macabre dance to keep their spirits up. As the sun shines down with cheerful indifference, and sharks crowd hopefully round the ship, the slave-trader prays:

> 'Oh, spare their lives for Jesus' sake
> Who did not die in vain!
> For if I don't keep three hundred head
> My business is down the drain.' (D 707; 6:199)

Poetry can do nothing to change this desolate world. In 'The God Apollo' a young nun leaves her convent in search of a wandering musician whom she has heard singing seductively in the guise of Phoebus Apollo, the god of poetry. From an old Jew she learns that her supposed Apollo is really Rabbi Faibisch, a former cantor in the Amsterdam synagogue, who now roams the country with a gaggle of prostitutes (6:32). Poetry is illusion. It creates a 'blessed secret world' in which the poet is 'king in the realm of thought' and 'ruler of a dream-world' (6:134-6). The poet, like the king, belongs to a vulnerable élite: 'in art as in life, the people can kill us, but never judge us' (6:135). Poetry is a winged horse (6:136) or a magic ship (6:247-8). Heine no longer communes with the elemental spirits inhabiting nature. 'The sky is desolate, a blue churchyard, silent and without divinity' (6:83), like the post-Newtonian universe in Schiller's 'The Gods of Greece'. Instead, the poet has to recreate nature with extreme artifice. This is conveyed in 'Jehuda ben Halevy' when the stories of the *aggadah*, which nourished Jehuda's imagination during his Talmud study, are compared to the hanging gardens of Babylon: an artificial paradise, suspended above the ground by technical skill. For the late Heine, poetry has again become the private world of imagination from which, at the outset of his career, he made such efforts to escape.

In the *Hebrew Melodies*, the last section of *Romancero*, Heine celebrates the three great Jewish poets of medieval Spain: Judah Halevi (whom Heine miscalls 'Jehuda Halevy'), Moses ibn Ezra, and Solomon ibn Gabirol. In this poem Heine inserts himself into the Jewish tradition of lamentation in exile. At prominent points he quotes from Psalm 137: 'By the rivers of Babylon, there we sat down, yea we wept when we remembered Zion' (cf. 6:135); 'If I forget thee, O Jerusalem, let my right hand forget her cunning [and] let my tongue cleave to the roof of my mouth' (cf. 6:129). But he associates himself more covertly with a German poet: Goethe. When he attributes his melancholy to 'my dark west-eastern spleen' (6:136) he is alluding to his dual German and Jewish allegiance but also to Goethe's book of Oriental poetry, the *West-Eastern Divan* (*West-östlicher Divan*). And just as Goethe in that book adopted the persona of the Persian poet Hafiz, so Heine here identifies with the Jewish poet Judah Halevi, in a complex act of cultural self-affirmation.

The covert presence of Goethe does something, but not much, to alleviate the pessimism with which Heine regards the poet's fate. Poets, he tells us, are naturally unlucky. Their character is summed up by the Jewish-German word *schlemiel*. Apollo, who pursued the nymph Daphne and found himself embracing a laurel-tree instead, was 'the divine schlemiel' (6:153). Heine tells the story of the original *schlemiel* by adapting an incident from the Old Testament. In Numbers 25, Zimri offends the Israelites by retiring to his tent with a Midianite woman, and Phinehas stabs them both with a javelin. But oral tradition, according to Heine, claims that Phinehas's javelin missed the guilty pair and instead struck an innocent bystander, Schlemiel ben Zuri Shaddai (6:155). This unfortunate character was the ancestor of all subsequent *schlemiels*, and hence of all poets. Similarly, Judah Halevi was casually killed by a passing Saracen while mourning on the ruins of Jerusalem. It is typical of a poet-*schlemiel* that, while another man enjoys a woman's favours, the poet blunders into the path of a missile meant for someone else.

Heine thus ends with two complementary images of the poet. In the dream-world of poetry, the poet reigns as an absolute monarch. In the real world of conflict and greed, the poet is a *schlemiel*, fated always to be defeated without dignity. Heine implies that if the poet is excluded from fame and fortune, that is not because the world is ill-disposed towards him: the world simply does not care. Thus Heine anticipates Thomas Mann's view of the artist as the perpetual outsider, and conveys the sense of marginality felt by poets in what Hegel called the age of prose. But the image of the poet as *schlemiel* also suggests more complex feelings. There is bitterness in it, and self-pity, but also a rather attractive self-deprecation which is not common in Heine's writings. It resembles the mood of Kafka's last story, *Josefine the Singer*, likewise written during its author's terminal illness, in which art is embodied in a singing mouse whose performances, though highly valued by the mice, are shown to be superfluous in their lives.

It is not the least astonishing thing about Heine that, prostrated by terrible illness, he could combine Jewish and German traditions to produce this complex and humorous statement about the art to which his life had been dedicated. The image of the poet as *schlemiel* is not Heine's last word, though. He has no last word, no final message transcending the antinomies round which we have seen his thought restlessly circling.

NOTES

1 : *Poetry versus Politics*

1 Immanuel Kant, *The Critique of Judgement*, tr. J. C. Meredith (Oxford: Clarendon Press, 1952), pp. 43–4.

2 Johann Wolfgang Goethe, *Dichtung und Wahrheit*, in *Sämtliche Werke* (40 vols., Frankfurt: Deutscher Klassiker Verlag, 1985–), I.xiv.631.

3 G. W. F. Hegel, *Aesthetics*, tr. T. M. Knox (Oxford: Clarendon Press, 1975), p. 103.

4 For Hegel's remarks on Dutch painting, see *ibid.*, pp. 162–3, 598–9, 885–7; on Sterne, *ibid.*, p. 602.

5 *Ibid.*, p. 1052.

6 For a partial translation, see Johann Gottfried Herder, 'Extract from a Correspondence on Ossian and the Songs of Ancient Peoples', in *German Aesthetic and Literary Criticism: Winckelmann, Lessing, Hamann, Herder, Schiller and Goethe*, ed. H. B. Nisbet (Cambridge: Cambridge University Press, 1985), pp. 154–61; see also R. T. Clark, *Herder: His Life and Thought* (Berkeley and Los Angeles: University of California Press, 1955).

7 Hegel, *Aesthetics*, p. 1092.

8 Arthur Schopenhauer, *The World as Will and Representation*, tr. E. J. Payne (2 vols., New York: Dover, 1969), i.312–13.

9 Friedrich Schiller, 'Die Götter Griechenlands', in *Werke*, ed. Gerhart Fricke and H. G. Göpfert (5 vols., Munich: Hanser, 1960), i.172.

10 Heine's word *Philister* has slightly different connotations from the English 'Philistine'. Originating from student slang, it implies petty and boring narrow-mindedness as well as smug contempt for anything unconventional.

11 Heinrich von Kleist, 'Katechismus der Deutschen', in *Sämtliche Werke und Briefe*, ed. Helmut Sembdner (2 vols., Munich: Hanser, 1961), ii.354.

12 Thomas Nipperdey, *Deutsche Geschichte 1800–1866* (Munich: Beck, 1983), p. 113.

13 Ludwig Börne, 'Goethes Briefwechsel mit einem Kind', in *Sämtliche Schriften*, ed. Peter and Inge Rippmann (5 vols., Düsseldorf: Melzer,

1964), ii.869; Wolfgang Menzel, *Die deutsche Literatur*, 2nd edn (4 vols., Stuttgart: Hallberger'sche Verlagshandlung, 1836), iii.343.

14 For an amusing account of such dramas, see Thomas Carlyle, 'Life and Writings of Werner', *in Critical and Miscellaneous Essays* (4 vols., London: Chapman & Hall, 1888), i.66–110.

15 Ludolf Wienbarg, *Ästhetische Feldzüge* (1834), quoted in Hartmut Steinecke, *Literaturkritik des Jungen Deutschland* (Berlin: Schmidt, 1982), p. 135.

16 Heine later reworked this passage and put it into the mouth of Ludwig Börne (4:15–16).

2 : The Spirit versus the Senses

1 'Lines written a few miles above Tintern Abbey' in *William Wordsworth*, ed. Stephen Gill (Oxford: Oxford University Press, 1984), p. 134.

2 G. W. F. Hegel, *Phenomenology of Spirit*, tr. A. V. Miller (Oxford: Oxford University Press, 1977), p. 17 (translation modified).

3 e.g. *Danton's Death*, I, v, in *The Plays of Georg Büchner*, tr. Victor Price (Oxford: Oxford University Press, 1971), p. 20; Alexander Herzen, *From the Other Shore*, tr. Moura Budberg (Oxford: Oxford University Press, 1979), p. 50. The phrase became proverbial during the French Revolution.

4 Hegel, *The Philosophy of History*, tr. J. Sibree (New York: Dover, 1956), p. 447.

5 *Hegel's Philosophy of Right*, tr. T. M. Knox (Oxford: Clarendon Press, 1942), p. 150.

6 Leszek Kolakowski, *Main Currents of Marxism* (3 vols., Oxford: Clarendon Press, 1978), i.92. This view has been spread in the English-speaking world especially by Bertrand Russell and Karl Popper. For rebuttals, see T. M. Knox, 'Hegel and Prussianism', in Walter Kaufmann (ed.), *Hegel's Political Philosophy* (New York: Atherton Press, 1970), pp. 13–29, and Walter Kaufmann, 'The Hegel Myth and its Method', in Alasdair MacIntyre (ed.), *Hegel: A Collection of Critical Essays* (Notre Dame: University of Notre Dame Press, 1976), pp. 21–60.

7 *Philosophy of Right*, p. 10.

8 'Towards a Critique of Hegel's *Philosophy of Right*: Introduction', in Karl Marx, *Selected Writings*, ed. David McLellan (Oxford: Oxford University Press, 1977), p. 63.

9 'Theses on Feuerbach', *ibid.*, p. 158.

10 'Towards a Critique of Hegel...', *ibid.*, p. 67.

11 Henri Saint-Simon, *Selected Writings on Science, Industry and Social Organisation*, tr. and ed. Keith Taylor (London: Croom Helm,

1975), p. 267 (translation modified).

12 Friedrich Nietzsche, 'The Genealogy of Morals', in *The Portable Nietzsche*, ed. Walter Kaufmann (New York: Viking, 1971), p. 453 (translation modified).

13 See Herbert Marcuse, *Eros and Civilization* (Boston: Beacon Press, 1955).

14 Heine quotes (3:677) what the Devil said when carrying off the black magician Pope Sylvester: 'Tu non pensavi ch'io loico fossi' ('You did not realize I was a logician')—Dante, *Inferno*, canto 27, line 123. Heine wrongly refers the reader to canto 28.

15 'The Gay Science', *The Portable Nietzsche*, pp. 95–6.

16 F. W. J. Schelling, *Ideen zu einer Philosophie der Natur*, in *Werke*, ed. Manfred Schröter (12 vols., Munich: Beck, 1927), i.706.

17 'An Answer to the Question: "What is Enlightenment?"' in *Kant's Political Writings*, ed. Hans Reiss, tr. H. B. Nisbet (Cambridge: Cambridge University Press, 1970), p. 54.

18 In placing food and drink at the centre of his utopia, Heine anticipates the work of the Russian scholar and philosopher Mikhail Bakhtin. Bakhtin argued that the prominence of the body and of eating and drinking in popular festivals, especially carnival, was an image of the good life with revolutionary and utopian implications: see Mikhail Bakhtin, *Rabelais and his World*, tr. Helene Iswolsky (Cambridge, Mass.: M.I.T. Press, 1968).

3 : *Between Revolutions*

1 *French Revolutionary Documents*, vol. i, ed. J. M. Roberts (Oxford: Blackwell, 1966), p. 172.

2 Donald Greer, *The Incidence of the Terror during the French Revolution: A statistical interpretation* (Cambridge, Mass.: Harvard University Press, 1935), p. 26. Greer points out (p. 27) that during the suppression of the Paris Commune in 1871, between fifteen and seventeen thousand Communards were executed in a single week. On the life of the majority in pre-revolutionary times, see Olwen Hufton, *The Poor of Eighteenth-Century France, 1750–1789* (Oxford: Clarendon Press, 1974).

3 Barrington Moore, Jr., *Social Origins of Dictatorship and Democracy* (Boston: Beacon Press, 1966), p. 104.

4 André Jardin and André-Jean Tudesq, *Restoration and Reaction, 1815–1848*, tr. Elborg Forster (Cambridge: Cambridge University Press, 1983), p. 99.

5 Roger Magraw, *France 1815–1914: The Bourgeois Century* (London: Fontana, 1983), p. 68.

6 Speech in the Chamber of Deputies, 1 March 1841, quoted in Jardin

HEINE

and Tudesq, p. 132.

7 'The Class Struggles in France' in Marx, *Selected Writings*, p. 286; this judgement is examined and confirmed by Roger Price, *The French Second Republic* (London: Batsford, 1972).

8 Quoted in Magraw, p. 85.

9 See David Cannadine, 'The Context, Performance and Meaning of Ritual: The British Monarchy and the "Invention of Tradition", c.1820–1977', in Eric Hobsbawm and Terence Ranger (eds.), *The Invention of Tradition* (Cambridge: Cambridge University Press, 1983), pp. 101–64.

10 Giorgio Tonelli, *Heine e la Germania* (Palermo: Istituto di Storia, 1963), p. 65.

11 See Walter Benjamin's essays on nineteenth-century Paris in *Charles Baudelaire: A Lyric Poet in the Era of High Capitalism*, tr. Harry Zohn and Quintin Hoare (London: New Left Books, 1973); Albrecht Betz, 'Commodity and Modernity in Heine and Benjamin', *New German Critique*, 33 (Fall 1984), 179–88.

12 Price, pp. 86–7; Jardin and Tudesq, p. 196.

13 Friedrich Engels, *The Condition of the Working Class in England in 1844*, tr. W. O. Henderson and W. H. Chaloner (Oxford: Blackwell, 1958), p. 149. Engels's habitual optimism made him an unreliable prophet: see Rosemary Ashton, *Little Germany: Exile and Asylum in Victorian England* (Oxford: Oxford University Press, 1986).

14 H. Schwab-Felisch, *Gerhart Hauptmann, 'Die Weber': Dichtung und Wirklichkeit* (Frankfurt and Berlin: Ullstein, 1963), p. 78.

15 Filippo Buonarroti, *Conspiration pour l'égalité, dite de Babeuf*, ed. Georges Lefebvre (2 vols., Paris: Éditions Sociales, 1957), ii.95, 96.

16 *Ibid.*, i. 99.

17 'Economic and Philosophical Manuscripts' in Marx, *Selected Writings*, p. 88.

18 'Towards a Critique of Hegel...', *ibid.*, p. 64.

19 Heine, *Deutschland: A not so sentimental journey*, tr. T. J. Reed (London: Angel Books, 1986), p. 30.

20 'Rapid Progress of Communism in Germany', by 'An Old Friend of Yours in Germany' [i.e. Engels], in *The New Moral World and Gazette of the Rational Society*, 13 Dec. 1844, p. 200.

21 This may be an inaccurate recollection of Exodus 12, where the houses marked with blood are those whose first-born children are to be spared; or, as A. I. Sandor suggests in *The Exile of Gods* (The Hague: Mouton, 1967), p. 95, it may recall how the French Catholics marked the doors of Huguenots before the massacre of St Bartholomew's Night in 1572.

22 Quoted in Louis Chevalier, *Labouring Classes and Dangerous Classes*

106

during the First Half of the Nineteenth Century, tr. Frank Jellinek (London: Routledge & Kegan Paul, 1973), p. 364.

23 George Rudé, *The Crowd in History*, 2nd edn (London: Lawrence & Wishart, 1981), pp. 175–7.

24 *The Recollections of Alexis de Tocqueville*, tr. A. T. de Mattos (London: Harvill, 1948), pp. 161, 197.

25 Heine's ambivalence before 1848 deserves comparison with the agonized reflections after the June repression by the exiled Russian revolutionary Herzen: see *From the Other Shore*, especially pp. 66–7.

26 'The Eighteenth Brumaire of Louis Bonaparte', in Marx, *Selected Writings*, p. 300.

4: *Between Religions*

1 Moses Mendelssohn, *Jerusalem*, in *Gesammelte Schriften* (17 vols., Berlin: Jüdischer Verlag; Stuttgart: Frommann, 1929–), viii.166.

2 Karl Marx, 'On the Jewish Question', in *Selected Writings*, p. 58.

3 Jakob Friedrich Fries, 'On the Danger to the Well-Being and Character of the Germans presented by the Jews' (1816), in *The Jew in the Modern World: A Documentary History*, ed. Paul R. Mendes-Flohr and Jehuda Reinharz (New York: Oxford University Press, 1980), p. 259.

4 See also Heine's portrait of the Frankfurt ghetto (4:21-7), and Steven E. Aschheim, *Brothers and Strangers: The East European Jew in German and German Jewish Consciousness, 1800–1923* (Madison, Wis.: University of Wisconsin Press, 1982).

5 The comparison with Kaufmann is made by S. S. Prawer, *Heine's Jewish Comedy* (Oxford: Clarendon Press, 1983), p. 90; on Oppenheim, see Ismar Schorsch, 'Art as Social History: Moritz Oppenheim and the German Jewish Vision of Emancipation', in Isadore Twersky (ed.), *Danzig, Between East and West: Aspects of Modern Jewish History* (Cambridge, Mass.: Harvard University Press, 1985), pp. 141–72.

6 Moses Hess, *Rom und Jerusalem* (Leipzig: Eduard Wengler, 1862), p. 4.

7 See Gershom Scholem, *The Messianic Idea in Judaism* (London: Allen & Unwin, 1971), p. 14.

8 Edward Gibbon, *The Decline and Fall of the Roman Empire* (6 vols., London: Dent, 1910), i.431.

9 Heine is alluding to Harriet Beecher Stowe, *Uncle Tom's Cabin* (1852). For Messalina, see Tacitus, *Annals*, Book 9.

10 Homer, *The Odyssey*, tr. Walter Shewring (Oxford: Oxford University Press, 1980), p. 139 (Book 11); Sophocles, *Oedipus at Colonus*, tr. Robert Fitzgerald, in *The Complete Greek Tragedies*

(New York: Random House, n.d.), iii.156–7 (lines 1224–6).

[11] *Recollections of Wittgenstein*, ed. Rush Rhees (Oxford: Oxford University Press, 1984), p. 108.

FURTHER READING

All of Heine's poetry is available in an English translation with thorough annotations: *The Complete Poems of Heinrich Heine*, tr. Hal Draper (Oxford: Oxford University Press, 1982). Draper succeeds superbly in translating the satirical Heine, but his touch sometimes falters with the early lyrics. The absence from English poetry of an equivalent to Heine's folk-song tradition means that these poems generally sound insipid in translation. A good attempt is the selection translated by Louis Untermeyer, *The Poems of Heinrich Heine* (London: Cape, 1938). More successful, because the author does have a folk-song tradition to draw on, are Alexander Gray's translations into Scots, *Songs and Ballads, chiefly from Heine* (London: Grant Richards, 1920). T. J. Reed rivals and perhaps outdoes Draper in his translation of *Deutschland: A not so sentimental journey* (London: Angel Books, 1986).

Heine's prose has not yet found a translator to match Draper. The most comprehensive (though not complete) version, *The Works of Heinrich Heine*, tr. C. G. Leland and others (12 vols., London: Heinemann, 1891–1905) is dated and bowdlerized. Selections from this and other nineteenth-century translations are often reissued, but new translations are badly needed. Meanwhile, *Heinrich Heine: A Biographical Anthology*, ed. Hugo Bieber, with translations made or selected by Moses Hadas (Philadelphia: Jewish Publication Society of America, 1956), is a useful stop-gap, providing selections from poetry, prose works and letters, with linking commentary and explanatory notes.

Two classic essays provide good introductions to Heine: 'Heinrich Heine' in Matthew Arnold, *Lectures and Essays in Criticism*, ed. R. H. Super (Ann Arbor: University of Michigan Press, 1962), pp. 107–32; and 'German Wit: Heinrich Heine', in *Essays of George Eliot*, ed. Thomas Pinney (London: Routledge & Kegan Paul, 1963), pp. 216–54.

The many older biographies of Heine have been superseded by Jeffrey L. Sammons, *Heinrich Heine: A Modern Biography* (Princeton: Princeton University Press, 1979). For sense and scholarship on the vexed question whether Heine's love-poems were about either or both of his cousins, see William Rose, *The Early Love Poetry of Heinrich Heine: An Inquiry into Poetic Inspiration* (Oxford: Clarendon Press, 1962).

For commentary on the poetry, see S. S. Prawer, *Heine: Buch der Lieder* (London: Arnold, 1960), a much richer book than its modest format suggests, and the same author's comprehensive *Heine, the Tragic Satirist: A Study of the Later Poetry 1827–56* (Cambridge: Cambridge University Press, 1961). On *Atta Troll*, see also Nigel Reeves, 'Atta Troll and his Executioners: the political significance of Heinrich Heine's tragi-comic epic', *Euphorion*, 73 (1979), 388–409. A forthcoming book by Michael Perraudin examines originality and imitation in the early poems. Barker Fairley, *Heinrich Heine: An Interpretation* (Oxford: Clarendon Press, 1954), points out recurring images in the poetry and prose. Laura Hofrichter, *Heinrich Heine* (Oxford: Clarendon Press, 1963), is helpful.

The best general literary study is Jeffrey L. Sammons, *Heinrich Heine: The Elusive Poet* (New Haven: Yale University Press, 1969). Its many excellences include its path-breaking exploration of the subtleties of Heine's prose and its appreciation of the late poems. A. I. Sandor, *The Exile of Gods* (The Hague: Mouton, 1967), traces the theme of exile through a surprising range of Heine's works.

William Rose, *Heinrich Heine: Two Studies of his Thought and Feeling* (Oxford: Clarendon Press, 1956) sensitively discusses 'Heine's social and political attitude' and 'Heine's Jewish feeling'. Nigel Reeves, *Heinrich Heine: Poetry and Politics* (Oxford: Oxford University Press, 1974), is a masterly analysis of Heine's poetry in relation to his thought. His article 'Heine and the Young Marx', *Oxford German Studies*, 7 (1972–3), 44–97, demonstrates Heine's influence on Marx. Robert C. Holub, *Heinrich Heine's Reception of German Grecophilia* (Heidelberg: Winter, 1981), is an important and wide-ranging study of Heine's aesthetics. S. S. Prawer, *Frankenstein's Island: England and the English in the Writings of Heinrich Heine* (Cambridge: Cambridge University Press, 1986), is a pleasure to read.

On Heine as Jew, S. S. Prawer, *Heine's Jewish Comedy: A Study of his Portraits of Jews and Judaism* (Oxford: Clarendon Press, 1983) is exhaustive. Its most rewarding sections are the affectionate explications of Heine's evocations of Jewish life in *The Rabbi of Bacharach*, the *Hebrew Melodies*, and elsewhere. See also Israel Tabak, *Judaic Lore in Heine* (Baltimore: Johns Hopkins Press, 1948), and, on the situation of German Jews in Heine's day, Michael A. Meyer, *The Origins of the Modern Jew: Jewish Identity and European Culture in Germany, 1749–1824* (Detroit: Wayne State University Press, 1967); Julius Carlebach, *Karl Marx and the Radical Critique of Judaism* (London: Routledge & Kegan Paul, 1978); and the section on Heine in Sander L. Gilman, *Jewish Self-Hatred: Anti-Semitism and the Hidden Language of the Jews* (Baltimore: Johns Hopkins University Press, 1986).

On German literature in its social setting, see Eda Sagarra, *Tradition and Revolution: German Literature and Society 1830–1890* (London: Methuen, 1971). For political history, see William Carr, *A History of Germany*, 3rd edn (London: Arnold, 1987), chs. 1 and 2. On French culture in Heine's day, F. W. J. Hemmings, *Culture and Society in France, 1789–1848* (Leicester: Leicester University Press, 1987); and on French history, the volume in the Cambridge History of Modern France by André Jardin and André-Jean Tudesq, *Restoration and Reaction, 1815–1848*, tr. Elborg Forster (Cambridge: Cambridge University Press, 1983). For the European context, see E. J. Hobsbawm, *The Age of Revolution* (London: Weidenfeld & Nicolson, 1962).

For selections from German aesthetics, see the three volumes of *German Aesthetic and Literary Criticism*, edited respectively by David Simpson, Kathleen Wheeler and H. B. Nisbet (Cambridge: Cambridge University Press, 1984–5). On Classicism, see T. J. Reed, *The Classical Centre: Goethe and Weimar, 1775–1832* (Oxford: Clarendon Press, 1986). On Romanticism in general, see H. G. Schenk, *The Mind of the European Romantics* (London: Constable, 1966); the more ambitious study by M. H. Abrams, *Natural Supernaturalism: Tradition and Revolution in Romantic Literature* (New York: Norton, 1971); and for German Romanticism, the bibliographical essay by Glyn Tegai Hughes, *Romantic German Literature* (London: Arnold, 1979).

On philosophy, see Julian Roberts, *German Philosophy: An Introduction* (Cambridge: Polity Press, 1987). On Hegel, see either the excellent basic introduction by Peter Singer, *Hegel* (Oxford: Oxford University Press, 1983), or Charles Taylor's challenging *Hegel* (Cambridge: Cambridge University Press, 1975). For selections from his followers, see *The Young Hegelians: An Anthology*, ed. Lawrence S. Stepelevich (Cambridge: Cambridge University Press, 1983).

For German political thinking in Heine's time, see the anthology *The Political Thought of the German Romantics*, ed. H. S. Reiss (Oxford: Blackwell, 1955); Hans Kohn, *The Mind of Germany* (London: Macmillan, 1961); James J. Sheehan, *German Liberalism in the Nineteenth Century* (Chicago: University of Chicago Press, 1978).

On Saint-Simon and his followers, see F. E. and F. P. Manuel, *Utopian Thought in the Western World* (Oxford: Blackwell, 1979), pp. 590–640; for their influence in Germany, see E. M. Butler, *The Saint-Simonian Religion in Germany: A Study of the Young German Movement* (Cambridge: Cambridge University Press, 1926).

INDEX OF HEINE'S WORKS

INDEX